RAISING

THE

SALAD

BAR

RAISING THE SALAD BAR

BY CATHERINE WALTHERS

PHOTOGRAPHY BY ALISON SHAW

~ LAKE ISLE PRESS ~
NEW YORK

Published by:
Lake Isle Press, Inc.
16 West 32nd Street, Suite 10-B
New York, NY 10001
(212) 273-0796
E-mail: lakeisle@earthlink.net

Distributed to the trade by:
National Book Network, Inc.
4501 Forbes Boulevard, Suite 200
Lanham, MD 20706
1(800) 462-6420
www.nbnbooks.com

Library of Congress Control Number: 2007924523

ISBN-13: 978-1-891105-33-3

ISBN-10: 1-891105-33-7

Book and cover design: Ellen Swandiak
Editors: Katherine Trimble, Pimpila Thanaporn

This book is available at special sales discounts for bulk purchases as premiums or special editions, including customized covers. For more information, contact the publisher at (212) 273-0796 or by e-mail, lakeisle@earthlink.net

First edition
Printed in the United States of America

10 9 8 7 6 5 4 3 2 1

DEDICATION
In memory of Johnna Albi, cooking mentor and friend

ACKNOWLEDGMENTS

I'm very grateful to friends and colleagues who contributed some fantastic recipes to this book, thereby elevating it greatly: Chris Brown, natural foods cooking instructor in Rhode Island; Jan Buhrman of Kitchen Porch Catering on Martha's Vineyard; Linda Carucci, director of culinary programs at COPIA, the American Center for Food, Wine and Arts in Napa Valley; Cathi DiCocco of Café DiCocoa in Bethel, Maine; Karen Dutton, manager of Tea Lane Caterers on Martha's Vineyard; Didi Emmons of Haley House Bakery Café in Roxbury; Boston chef Burke Forster; Tina Miller, author of *Vineyard Harvest*; Christopher Osborn, former chef/owner of The Depot in Newton; Patti Powers and Ralph Legrande of Cheshire Garden in New Hampshire; Laura Silber, private chef on Martha's Vineyard; Michael Scott, head of the cheese department at the Newtonville Whole Foods Market; Boston Food writer Rachel Travers; Rachel Vaughn, private chef from Big Sky, Montana; and Job Yacubian of Bittersweet Restaurant on Martha's Vineyard.

A big thank you to friends who home tested these recipes and gave me great feedback: Ellen Blue, Sue Jensen, Pamela Florence, Bill and Betty Haynes, Karin Stanley, Brenda Wallis, Wendy Weldon and Susan White. A special thanks to Linda Thompson and Pat Kauffman for the significant number of recipes they tried.

A most enjoyable aspect of writing this book were the Friday lunches, where friends—and friends of friends—came to eat and critique. These food critics included Sarah Vail, Abby Webster, Laura Hall, Diana Gilmore, Sharon Eber, Sofya Nadelstein, Kathy Forsythe, Leslie Johnson, Sue Dawson, Hillary Noyes-Keene, Dee Dice, Ann Nelson, Deborah Silliman, and Chris Fielder, among others.

Bernie Cormie, who has tried nearly every salad in this book and is a regular at the Friday lunches, generously gave her time, ideas and support throughout. Thanks Bernie—let's do it again.

I always find support and good cheer from the Ladies Who Lunch: Boston food writers Clara Silverstein, Carolyn Faye Fox, Andrea Pyenson, Rachel Travers, Lise Stern, and Lisa Zwirn, and more support from the MV ladies who write: Kate Feiffer, Niki Patton, Janet Holladay, Laura Roosevelt and Wendy Palmer. Special thanks to Jamie Stringfellow, former editor of *Martha's Vineyard Magazine*, for her many talents and friendship, and longtime friend Jacquie Clermont of Amberheart design.

My agent Clare Pelino is wonderful and I am grateful for her time and talent that led to the creation of this book. My appreciation to Hiroko Kiiffner, publisher of Lake Isle Press, Kate Trimble for all her work and positive attitude, and Ellen Swandiak for the book's beautiful design.

I felt extremely lucky to be able to work with Vineyard photographer Alison Shaw, whom I knew would be the perfect person to bring these colorful salads to life. She also loves to cook and tested a number of the recipes.

When photographing the salads, Mark Weiner of Martha's Vineyard Glassworks generously lent us some of the studio's beautiful hand-blown bowls and plates.

Thanks to the growers on MV who, whether they realize it or not, keep me inspired with their fresh and wonderful food: the folks at Morning Glory Farm, Debby Farber of Blackwater Farm, Lisa Fisher of Stannard Farms, Marie and Andrea Scott at Beetlebung Farm; Krishana Collins of Bluebird Way Farm (who grew the arugula shown in the cover photo), the Nortons at Bayes Norton Farm, Andrew Woodruff of Whippoorwill Farm and CSA and everyone at the West Tisbury Farmers Market. I'd like to add Louie Larsen of the Net Result, who is always helpful in answering my questions about seafood (as well as providing the best fish around).

My husband David, and son James, 8, tested every recipe—sometimes several times throughout one winter. We always had a few laughs with our salad-rating system.

HOW THIS BOOK CAME ABOUT

 For the past twelve years, I have worked as a private chef in peoples' homes, cooking for clients and stocking up meals on a weekly basis. Each week, I have the challenge of coming up with something new.

Sometimes I'd find myself becoming complacent about salads, thinking that perhaps others didn't really care if the salad, the perennial supporting actor, were interesting or not. I gravitated toward shortcuts, using the pre-washed, mixed baby greens and serving them with a good vinaigrette. This way, I thought I might save more time for main dishes such as short ribs with a wine sauce or salmon wrapped in Napa cabbage. Nobody seemed to complain.

But there was only so much to be done with pre-mixed greens, and I soon returned to putting together my own salads, pairing arugula with butterhead lettuce, or watercress with endive, adding fruits or vegetables in season like grapefruit, blueberries, pears, pomegranate seeds and daikon radishes; and experimenting with different cheeses or vinegars and oils. Like magic, while no one had previously noticed or said anything about my salads, I began to get compliments. "That salad was really good last week," or "I like the fresh fruit with greens." It showed me that given some attention, salads can be rewarding dishes, as good or even better than the short ribs or salmon. And because I've always been a salad and vegetable lover, I treat the salad course with the same detailed attention I give to preparing the entrees.

Along the way, especially during recent years, I noticed a number of new vinegars on the market. There have been big changes in this category, and while it has received little attention, I would say that the improvements are as compelling as the ones regarding olive oils. Whereas there used to be three or four basic choices in vinegars—mostly red, white and balsamic—there is now Cabernet or Zinfandel red wine vinegar, Champagne vinegars made from sparkling white wine and white balsamic made from California Chardonnay. And they are delicious! Producers of these artisanal vinegars, many based in California, approach vinegar-making the same way vintners seek to improve their wines—by looking at and evaluating every aspect of production.

These new, full-bodied flavors make great vinaigrettes. Researching this book gave me the excuse to try all kinds of interesting-looking vinegars. By the end, I had about 30 of them, and began offering vinegar tastings in some of my cooking classes. You needn't repeat my obsession, but I do recommend trying some new vinegars (see the vinaigrette chapter, page 233, for suggestions) and keeping a small collection—say three to five—on hand for the variety of options they present for salad making.

Wanting more fresh takes on salad, I started to consider traditional family recipes such as those for potato salad and chicken salad. Many families continue to make the same handed-down recipes, dating back decades. While there's nothing wrong with tradition, these salads haven't taken into account the vast changes in the availability of ingredients. Preparing a variety of different salads each week, every week of the year naturally led to a collection of favorites and the idea to write a comprehensive salad book. I've put together ten different chicken salads, and as many pasta and potato salads, in addition to lots of new ideas for leafy green salads for dinners, backyard barbecues, potlucks, picnics and other gatherings where food is the main event. When I was done, I knew that I myself would enjoy this new collection of delicious salad recipes.

I've added some new categories to the traditional ones, including bean and grain salads. The grain salads are particularly unique and people love them. I mix whole grains such as quinoa, wheat berries, barley and farro with vegetables, leafy greens and simple dressings to make a complete package. Best of all, they meet my ultimate standard for the kinds of dishes I like to create: those that contribute to good health and are delicious. I hope you enjoy these salad recipes as much as I've enjoyed developing them.

WAYS TO USE THIS BOOK

This book, like almost any cookbook, offers different things to different readers. For those who love salads, it offers new ideas and combinations, new ingredients and vinaigrettes. For those new to salad making, it offers the basics of how to make a vinaigrette, and a compendium of greens and techniques, such as how to prepare the most tender chicken for salads.

To make a merely good salad a great one, learn to make your own homemade dressings. They always taste better and fresher than the bottled versions. By using the tools, tips, and oil and vinegar recommendations, making dressings at home will become second nature to everyone.

There are really no rules for making salads. In fact, among their best qualities are how versatile and accommodating they can be. Measurements are necessary to create a recipe and provide general guidelines, but often, it's more fun to use your instincts and follow your own tastes. If it seems there are too many tomatoes in a salad, take some out. If you don't like shrimp in the Cajun Shrimp and Corn Salad, remove them and enjoy a great corn and tomato salad. If you can't find mâche lettuce or a daikon radish, substitute another green or similar vegetable such as red radish or carrot. If you don't have Champagne vinegar, use apple cider vinegar or rice vinegar instead. And so on.

Toward the end of writing this book, as I reviewed the recipes, I'd think of some changes I could make. "This would be a good combination," or "I'd make it this way now." Rather than thinking that salads could always be better, I realized that they're an ever-changing thing—and that's good. No two salads will ever be exactly the same, even if two people follow the same recipe to the letter. The vinegar and olive oil will be different, greens will come from varied sources, and depending on the time of year, the tomato will be sweeter.

A variety of ingredients, the familiar along with the new, is key to salad-making and this book. I noticed that when friends and family tested these recipes, almost everyone found a new ingredient or technique they could appreciate. One friend tried wheat berry salads for the first time and became an instant fan. Another discovered that Napa cabbage or bok choy could be used raw in salads, and that they are sweet and succulent. Still another had never tried jicama, and could see the benefit of having this crisp, juicy vegetable in her salad repertoire. As for me, I became enamored of edamame beans, and now love their clean, subtle taste and the crunch they add to salads with grains, beans and greens.

It's not always easy to think outside the box—or bowl—but it only takes discovering and using something once to make it familiar. Each time you do, you open the door to creative possibilities and head down the road to more adventurous cooking.

If I had to offer just one piece of advice for creating the most delicious salads (aside from making your own dressings and vinaigrettes) it would be to seek out fresh ingredients from the source. Consider joining a farm share program or visit a local farm stand of one of the 3,000 farmers markets across the country. Even better are ingredients that come from your own backyard garden. Buying locally raised foods is one of the most important trends happening today. Perhaps it's a response to the extent of corporate dominance over what we eat and the compromises implied therein, notably the absence of flavor in many of our supermarket foods, nowhere more noticeable than in a salad of leafy greens and vegetables.

During the winter as I was testing recipes for this book I relied on the supermarket for my ingredients. One day, a young farmer who had been invited to a Friday testing brought a salad mix grown in a local greenhouse. Wow! I realized that I had been settling for less. His greens were light and tender, I could "smell" the taste and I could differentiate the flavors of individual lettuces and greens. This quality mix of baby lettuces and greens by itself, with a simple dressing, made a perfect accompaniment to almost any dish.

TABLE OF CONTENTS

INTRODUCTION

If I had to pick just one word to describe the essence of a salad it would be "refreshing." Salads can be cooling or thirst-quenching in summer, or vibrant and alive amid heavier foods in winter. Salads are satisfying, full-flavored dishes that anyone can easily put together at home.

While salads may never reach the status of a grill-roasted beef tenderloin or a dense chocolate cake, they do have admirable attributes of their own, namely, the unadulterated goodness and flavors of their ingredients. Think of a really ripe strawberry, a fresh fig, a crunchy slice of garden cucumber, a just-picked tomato, a tender leaf of arugula. These, and dozens more, are the ingredients that are at our fingertips.

It's recommended that we eat a minimum of nine fruits and vegetables each day, and the salads in this book offer a great game plan to reach that goal. They feature fresh seasonal ingredients including dark leafy greens, brightly colored vegetables said to contain the most nutrients, and fresh fruits packed with antioxidants. Add to that some supercharged whole grains, fiber-rich beans and protein power from seafood, chicken and meat, and you can count on plenty of fresh, healthy food coming your way.

I've included every type of salad I could think of and make sure they are all brimming with fresh vegetables and fruits, leafy greens and herbs. These salads also reflect today's tastes and the increased availability of ingredients and ethnic influences at supermarkets and specialty stores. Updated chicken salads call for grilled, roasted or poached chicken with many different ingredients ranging from bok choy to roasted artichokes. I've included pasta salads full of herbs and vegetables, and leafy green salads with homemade vinaigrettes and other dressings. Vinaigrettes are among the new culinary stars, adding zest to otherwise unexciting dishes. Here they do double duty, serving as both light coatings for greens and vegetables and as sauces for chicken, beef or fish. Spicy Thai Steak with Napa Cabbage Salad, for instance, has a spicy lime dressing that flavors both the steak and the salad (page 99).

My goal for this book was to take salad beyond just a plate of leafy greens. I hope you think the following recipes do just that.

The outcome of a recipe can depend on a number of subtle things—the size of a cut vegetable, the type of pan used and, most importantly, the quality of ingredients. I've written a few notes on the latter that will, I hope, put us on the same page. You'll find additional information about specific ingredients in each of the chapters.

Salt

All of the recipes in this book were made and tested with Diamond brand kosher salt. Of the three basic salts (table, sea and kosher), kosher salt is the most ideal for salads. It dissolves faster—twice as fast, say some experts—and adheres to food better than regular table or sea salt does. And because of the larger size and shape of the salt crystals, it also has much less sodium per teaspoon than regular table salt. Sodium levels can also vary among different brands. I prefer the Diamond brand over Morton's kosher salt because it is lower in sodium and free of additives, which can sometimes produce a metallic flavor.

The differences in the sodium content of various salts make it difficult to specify accurate amounts of salt in a recipe. For this reason, most vinaigrettes and dressings suggest adding salt and pepper "to taste."

Salt, however, is an important flavoring agent, and brings out the best flavors in everything. So my advice is to be generous with it, adding in pinches until the flavors are fully drawn out. I'm not suggesting you make foods "salty," just flavorful. If something tastes bland, chances are it may only need a little salt.

In most dressings for a salad that serves 4, I typically use 2 or 3 pinches of kosher salt, or about 1/4 to 1/2 teaspoon. Bland foods like potatoes, grains and pasta usually require more salt. Always add some salt to the water when cooking whole grains and pastas to make them more flavorful (they absorb the salt during cooking).

Freshly Ground Black Pepper

Freshly ground pepper has a vibrant taste and a little bite, more so than pre-ground pepper which quickly loses its flavorful oils. I'm always surprised that many kitchens lack this simple ingredient, as it can add so much to so many dishes, including salads. It's worthwhile to invest in a good pepper mill.

Extra-Virgin Olive Oil

When a recipe calls for olive oil, in all cases it means extra-virgin olive oil, unless another type of oil such as canola is specified. Extra-virgin olive oil is pressed directly from olives, processed without chemicals or heat. It's better for you, and imparts more flavor to your salad. So-called "pure" or "light" olive oils are processed, and are bland, nearly devoid of taste. Among extra-virgin olive oils, however, flavors can range from mild to more pronounced, depending upon the olives used and

SALAD BASICS

where they were grown. For salads, I'd suggest a milder tasting extra-virgin olive oil without heavy overtones. It should blend nicely with a variety of ingredients and not overpower the other flavors in your salad. Have a taste test with friends or try one recommended in cooking magazine tests to find one that suits your taste. I am partial to an olive oil called Greek Gourmet.

Using Fresh Herbs

All fresh herbs should be rinsed before using. Many of them, such as parsley, dill and cilantro can be quite sandy or have pockets of dirt and need to be rinsed and dried before using. Fill a salad spinner or smaller herb spinner with cold water, swish the herbs around, lift, empty out the water and spin dry. Herbs like tarragon, chives, thyme and rosemary can be held under running water and dried on paper towels.

To store most leftover fresh herbs, wrap them in dry paper towels and put in a plastic bag, but don't close it tightly; refrigerate.

Celery

People usually have celery in the refrigerator and it makes a great addition to salads—crunchy, tasty and pretty. But it can sometimes be too crunchy or stringy and take a while to chew. For this reason, when using celery in a salad, I often peel the back of celery to remove the fibers. A Y-shaped vegetable peeler works best for this. After peeling, cut the celery stalks in half lengthwise and slice as thinly as possible—they should look like slivers.

Parmesan Cheese

In recipes that call for Parmesan cheese, I highly recommend the real thing, aged Parmigiano Reggiano, imported from Italy. Its flavor is bold and buttery, but not overly pungent or salty. It's very different from what comes in a can and more flavorful than domestic Parmesan brands. It is expensive, but a little goes a long way. Go for the flavor!

Dried Herbs and Spices

Dried herbs and spices generally have a shelf life of about 6 months. After that, they begin to lose potency. Try this test on your own: open a container and take a whiff; if you can't smell anything, chances are that you're adding nothing to your dish.

There may be other good spice sources, but I recommend Penzeys

Spices for several reasons. Their spices are very fresh, you'll find hard-to-locate ones such as ancho chili powder, and prices are reasonable. Their small, 1.25-ounce containers allow you to order minimal amounts of spices you use only occasionally and to sample some herbs or spices you haven't tried before (these small containers generally cost under $2).

If you want a heads-up on the spices I've used throughout this book and want to have them on hand, here are the ones I suggest from Penzeys: Cajun spice mix, sweet curry powder, ancho chili powder, chipotle chili powder, ground yellow mustard, sumac, red pepper flakes, ground cumin, Turkish oregano and dried wasabi powder. One that I didn't use here that's also wonderful is smoked paprika.

Tomatoes

I suggest using fresh tomatoes, only when they are in season, purchased at a farmers market or farm stand. Supermarket tomatoes generally look nice, but have little to no taste and often have an unpleasant mealy texture. There are some exceptions, but rarely. During the off-season, I generally use cherry tomatoes, which are sweet, juicy and moderately flavorful year-round.

Avoid storing tomatoes in the refrigerator, either whole or chopped in a salad. Refrigeration destroys one of the tomato's key flavor components and makes the texture mealy.

Olives

Use fresh olives whenever possible. Most cheese or deli counters sell dozens of different olives packed in brine or oil, from tiny French Niçoise olives to Greek kalamatas. Use these rather than the canned variety which usually don't have much flavor. Pitted fresh olives are generally more convenient, if a bit more costly.

Maple Syrup and Honey

I like to use pure maple syrup, not maple-flavored breakfast syrup. It has a mellow flavor that effortlessly melds into a dressing. You can substitute regular sugar or honey, but use slightly less if you do.

When using honey, I try to find raw honey or local honey sources. These tend to have mellower flavors that blend more harmoniously with other ingredients rather than intrude with a too-strong honey taste.

Citrus

When a recipe calls for "fresh" lemon, lime or orange juice, this means freshly squeezed from the fruit. Avoid bottled lime or lemon juices, or packaged orange juice; the real thing tastes much better.

Panko Breadcrumbs

Panko, Japanese-style breadcrumbs, make a uniquely crispy coating for chicken, fish, tomatoes for pan-frying and many other uses. They're extra-crispy because the bread they are made from is "shaved" into shard-like pieces, rather than ground as are regular breadcrumbs. Look for panko breadcrumbs in the Asian section of the supermarket, or at an Asian grocery store. Brands do vary; choose ones that have the smallest, most even crumbs.

If you can't find panko breadcrumbs, making your own in the food processor using French or Italian bread also works nicely: place un-toasted bread (without crusts) in the food processor and process for about 1 minute until crumbs form.

Use these tips as guidelines for prepping ingredients.

Making Croutons

Homemade croutons add great flavor and satisfying crunch to salads. You'll want to have a lot of these on hand—they're very popular.

1 medium-size Italian, French, or sourdough loaf, crusts removed, cut into cubes (about 3 cups)
2 tablespoons olive oil
1 teaspoon finely minced garlic
Salt and pepper

Preheat the oven to 350°. Place the bread cubes in a bowl and toss them with olive oil and garlic; season with salt and pepper. Place the cubes on a baking sheet and toast them in the oven for 10 to 12 minutes, or until the bread is slightly crisp and brown but still soft on the inside. You can substitute 1 tablespoon melted butter for 1 tablespoon olive oil or toss in fresh herbs like chopped parsley or rosemary.

Roasting Red Bell Peppers

To roast a red bell pepper, place it directly over a gas burner with the flame turned to high. Char the outside of the pepper, turning as needed with tongs. When the pepper is charred (completely black), place it in a brown paper bag and close it to "steam" or "sweat" for about 10 minutes or until it is cool enough to handle. Peel off the charred exterior, then remove the core and seeds, and rinse if necessary to remove any leftover blackened pieces.

If you have an electric stove, place the whole pepper under the broiler and char it the same way, turning with tongs to blacken.

Cutting Matchsticks

Cutting carrots and other vegetables into matchsticks always looks great in salads and makes them easier to chew.

Choose a thick carrot and peel it. Cut the carrot on a sharp diagonal into thin oval slices. Stack 2 or 3 slices and cut them into 1/8-inch wide strips.

Use this method for cutting radishes and daikon into matchsticks as well.

Toasting Nuts

The flavor of most nuts and seeds intensifies when they're toasted, especially walnuts, pecans, sliced almonds, hazelnuts, cashews and sesame seeds. I like pine nuts either way, toasted or untoasted.

Preheat the oven or toaster oven to 350°. Place nuts on a baking sheet and bake until lightly toasted and fragrant, usually about 6 to 9 minutes, depending on the kind of nut or seed. Remove from oven and cool. Take care to avoid burning, which can happen very quickly, and use a timer, because it's easy to forget. By the time you smell the nuts, they're usually burned.

Sectioning Oranges and Grapefruits

With a sharp knife, remove the peel and pith from the fruit, first by cutting off the top and bottom, then slicing off the sides along its contours. Trim off any remaining pith, which is bitter. Cut between the fruit segments and membranes to remove each section. Save the pulpy membrane—it's full of juice and is sometimes used in dressings.

Seeding a Cucumber

Cucumber seeds can add additional unwanted moisture to a salad, though it's really a matter of taste.

After peeling the cucumber, cut it lengthwise down the middle. Use a spoon or a melon baller to scrape out the seeds. Then cut as recipe directs.

Dicing a Mango

Remove mango skin with a paring knife or Y-shaped peeler. Slice a little off the larger end of the mango so you can hold the fruit upright. Cut slices about 1/4-inch thick down on either side of the pit. You should get 2 or 3 slices, depending on the mango size. Cut each slice into 1/4-inch strips, and each strip into 1/4-inch dice.

Mincing Garlic and Ginger

When mincing garlic for dressings, it's best to mince as finely as possible, reaching a consistency that's actually closer to a paste. This way the garlic flavor disperses evenly throughout the dressing or vinaigrette and you'll avoid getting bites of raw garlic. I mention this because in my cooking classes when I ask students to "finely mince" garlic, it usually shows up chopped, and I have to send them back 2 or 3 times before it's actually minced.

It helps to add a pinch of kosher salt to garlic while mincing—it draws moisture out, and helps prevent the garlic from sticking to your knife as you chop. Sometimes I use the food processor if I need to mince a large amount of garlic (the same goes for ginger).

A good tool for finely grating fresh ginger is a microplane-type zester. (You can find them in housewares stores.) These work well for grating garlic and shallots too.

Corn off the Cob

Fresh corn kernels have a sweet crunch that is not always typical of frozen corn niblets. Go for the fresh version whenever possible. It's a colorful, delicious addition to so many salads.

Removing the kernels from the cob is easy: after stripping off the husks and silk, stand the ear on one end in a large bowl. With a sharp knife, slice down the cob from top to bottom, right along the edge. The kernels will neatly fall into the bowl.

Opening an Avocado

The best avocado for salads is one that is just ripe, not overripe or soft. It slices better and looks better. The outside should be somewhat firm but yield slightly when pressed with your finger or thumb.

To open an avocado cut it in half lengthwise, through to the pit. Separate the halves by twisting them in separate directions. Remove the pit either by hitting it with the blade of your knife and twisting it out or by scooping it out with a spoon.

After removing the pit, scoop the flesh out from each side in one piece with a large spoon such as a soup spoon. Then you can slice or dice it.

Opening a Pomegranate

I've tried many different methods suggested for opening a pomegranate, but the best one came from Abe, an employee at my local Whole Foods Market who originally hails from Egypt. With a paring knife, cut a circle the size of a quarter around the top and bottom ends of the pomegranate and remove each circle. Use the knife to score the fruit on the outside in 4 even quarters, just cutting through the thin red peel, not through to the seeds. Open the fruit into quarters, and remove the seeds from each quarter over a bowl. Discard any white pith.

LIGHT LEAFY GREENS

LIGHT LEAFY GREENS

Essentially, there are two elements in a salad: greens and a vinaigrette. For salad greens, as with other ingredients, quality is crucial to the overall taste of the dish, which is why you should head straight to their source. Farm-grown lettuces and other leafy greens, available at farmers markets, roadside farm stands or through farm share programs, can be meltingly tender and full of variety and flavor. These greens have taste, because that's what they are grown for, unlike supermarket greens raised with shipping and shelf life in mind. Tossed with a homemade vinaigrette, these simply make the best salads. While you're shopping, you can pick up other salad fixings: colorful heirloom and cherry tomatoes, garden-grown cucumbers, fragrant herbs—all are secrets of a good salad chef.

One favorite source that I frequent on Martha's Vineyard is a self-serve organic farm stand at Beetlebung Corner, where bags of mixed baby greens picked that morning are displayed in ice-cold water. I can even see a few colorful edible flowers poking through the greens, each leaf of which maintains its own character and flavor. No matter what else I add or which dressing I create, I'm assured a failsafe, perfect salad every time. My other stop is the West Tisbury Farmers Market held each Saturday. Here, I find multiple choices: Asian salad mixes, zesty micro-greens, bright beautiful heads of lettuce, and my salad staple, arugula. Several of the growers offer bags of tiny baby arugula. At this stage, it's so tender, fragrant and deliciously peppery, that it tastes exquisite with just about everything from grilled peaches to shrimp, or just a slice of your favorite cheese.

At the other end of the spectrum, prepackaged supermarket salad mixes often taste bland by comparison. This is when a tasty dressing comes in handy, because you might not taste much else. These greens are shipped around the country and must be prepared for the trip. Some are dipped in chlorine, washing the flavor away. Some are grown for hardiness, like some baby greens I've tried which taste more like cardboard than lettuce.

In the winter, when local farm lettuces are unavailable, some supermarket greens work better than others. Romaine lettuce remains crunchy and fresh-tasting when it's buoyed by a Greek-style vinaigrette or a lemony dressing. Peppery arugula and watercress retain their flavors, and offer topnotch nutrients as well. Some loose leaf or butterhead varieties remain mild and tender. Aside from dressings, winter salads can benefit from the addition of seasonal fruits and vegetables like oranges, mangoes and grapefruit for flavor.

Becoming familiar with the variety of lettuces and greens and understanding their qualities can help you create many different salads.

Arugula

Spicy, nutty and peppery, arugula has a character all its own that contributes vivid flavor to a salad, as its many admirers will attest. Its flavor and dark green color make it the perfect green to mix with and enhance mellower greens like Boston, bibb or loose leaf lettuces. It also makes a colorful presentation when paired with radicchio or endive. Arugula's peppery flavor makes it a natural balance for sweet fresh figs, pomegranates, apples, watermelon, strawberries, raspberries, grilled apricots, tomatoes and citrus, as well as mild, sweet dressings such as raspberry or balsamic vinaigrettes. It partners equally well with the salty notes of olives and prosciutto, and either sharp or creamy cheeses, especially goat cheese, blue cheese and Parmesan. It's truly the renaissance green of the salad world, and best of all it's the most nutritious: high in calcium, beta-carotene and vitamin C, among other health boosters.

Butterhead, Boston and Bibb Lettuces

Butterhead encompasses both Boston and bibb lettuces. Their soft, velvety leaves have a mild, pleasantly delicate, buttery flavor. The pale green outer leaves and cream-colored yellow centers pair perfectly with darker, spicier greens like arugula, watercress and radicchio. Dressings that enhance these delicate lettuces might include a balsamic vinaigrette, a fruity Champagne or grapefruit vinaigrette, or a dressing with plenty of herbs. Try Boston or bibb lettuce with pears or pomegranate seeds in the fall, with a citrus-based vinaigrette in winter, and with roasted apricots or watermelon chunks in the summer. Top with tangy goat cheese and/or toasted nuts.

The Chicories: Endive, Frisée, Radicchio, Chicory and Dandelion

The pleasantly bitter members of the chicory family often act as supporting actors in salads. In the case of frisée, the curly, crisp leaves lend sharp texture to contrast with smoother greens like butterhead. Frisée stands up well in warm salads, and can also be used in chicken salads, potato salads and pasta salads when you want to add a touch of green or a contrasting texture.

Radicchio sports a unique, beautiful cranberry and white color combo that brightens salads made with light and dark greens. Try cutting radicchio into thin shreds to scatter color throughout a salad and disperse its slightly bitter taste. Radicchio can be soaked in cold water for 10 to 15 minutes to reduce some of its bitterness, if desired. Partner radicchio with arugula, loose leaf and butter lettuces or endive, and add berries, cheese, nuts, chicken or smoked meats.

Cut endive leaves crosswise or lengthwise into strips and add them to salads for a striking presentation. Their pale yellow and white leaves make a nice contrast to darker greens and can lighten a dish. Try adding endive to chicken, grain and pasta salads as well.

Chicory and escarole can have overly strong flavors and a tough texture that aren't favorable for salads.

True dandelion greens are hard to find, and often what you get in the supermarket is a type of chicory rather than a tender, young dandelion green that tastes delicious in a salad. Dandelion is inherently bitter, but that bitterness can be tamed by the addition of olive oil, cheese, eggs, garlic, lemon juice, tomatoes or croutons to your salad.

Loose Leaf Lettuces

These lovely lettuces includes green leaf, red leaf, ruby, lollo rossa, tango—all full heads of large, loosely connected leaves, unlike more compact varieties. Because of their mild tastes, loose leaf lettuces have great versatility when it comes to pairing with vinaigrettes and various accompaniments.

Mâche

Mâche is a very tender green with delicate and small, round dark green leaves. Harvested in small bunches, it has a nutty flavor and velvety texture. It is highly perishable, often expensive, and should be used the day it's bought and dressed just before serving. Mâche can be dressed by itself with a vinaigrette, or combined with radicchio, endive, bibb lettuce, beets and celery among other ingredients. Mâche can also be used as a garnish, lightly dressed, alongside a quiche or omelet; as well as with rice or potato dishes.

Mesclun or Mixed Baby Greens

Mesclun is a French term that means "mixture," specifically one consisting of tender young lettuce leaves and greens harvested at 3 to 6 weeks and combined with color, texture and flavor in mind. You can find the most interesting, flavorful mixes at farmers markets. They are often now referred to simply as mixed baby greens. These leaf mixes can stand on their own in salads because the greens are so varied. Prewashed and ready for the salad bowl, it's hard to beat them for convenience. Try all types of salad dressings with mesclun but especially the sweeter, lighter ones that balance the spicier greens in the mix, such as balsamic or raspberry vinaigrettes. Top mesclun salads with toasted nuts or seeds, including sunflower seeds, walnuts, pecans, pine nuts and your favorite cheese. You can also use mesclun mixes as a base for chicken or potato salad.

Micro-Greens

Now that we appreciate and crave baby greens of all kinds, make room for micro-greens. Harvested at under two weeks, these tiny greens can be measured in centimeters, but come with big, bright flavors and lots of nutrients. The micro field includes arugula, mustard greens, cilantro, mizuna, beet greens, fennel and kale, among others.

Like their variety, their uses are many: chefs use them mostly as edible garnishes for fish or other dishes, but they can offer splashy punches of flavor to pasta or potato salads, fruit salads, seafood salads and more. Some pairings seem inevitable: micro-beet greens in a dish with beets or micro-fennel with slivered fennel, micro-radish greens with radishes. Like sprouts, but less crunchy and more tender, micro-greens provide a textural and visually pleasant element to any number of dishes. They also make Alice-in-Wonderland-like salads on their own.

Chefs usually special order micro-greens, but some growers are beginning to package them like fresh herbs and are making them available in some markets. Also check your local farmers market for these remarkable miniatures.

Mizuna

A mustard green of Chinese origin, mizuna is a feathery, elegant leafy green with dark, serrated leaves. It's milder and less bracing than other mustard greens, but still offers good flavor. It's an unusual accent to salads in terms of both beautiful texture and mild mustard taste. It's also hardy—it won't easily wilt when dressed and therefore makes a good green to use in bean, grain, chicken and Asian noodle salads.

Pea Shoots

A true delicacy, pea shoots are the tendrils and top leaves of the snow pea plant. Tender and delicious, with fresh pea flavor, they can be used raw in salads and dressed as a bed for fish or chicken. They should be dressed at the very last minute before serving.

Romaine Lettuce

Thick, crisp, juicy romaine is one of today's most versatile and popular salad greens. Its fresh flavor is especially welcome during winter months. The sturdy leaves work well with many vegetables from radishes and cucumbers to tomatoes, avocados and red onions. With romaine, you can use bolder dressings such as blue cheese, Greek and Italian herb dressings, Green Goddess and, of course, Caesar. Different varieties include red or speckled romaine which make a colorful presentation when mixed with all-green romaine. In addition to Parmesan cheese, it also holds up well with blue cheese and feta.

Spinach

Mild-tasting and versatile, the emergence of bagged and boxed baby spinach has increased this leafy green's popularity in today's marketplace. In salads, it tastes terrific with olives, anchovies, garlic, tomatoes, red onions, daikon radishes, red bell peppers, carrots, citrus, pears, fennel, bacon, ham, eggs and cheeses, especially sharp, tangy ones like feta, goat cheese and Parmesan. Dressings made with lemon, mustard or red wine vinegar are ideal spinach partners.

Spinach is high in vitamins A, C and E—the antioxidant vitamins said to promote good health. It is also one of the highest sources of carotenoids (a family that includes beta carotenes), and contains iron, calcium and folic acid.

Watercress

With its slightly spicy, peppery leaves, watercress is perky and vibrant on its own or when paired with milder lettuces such as bibb, Boston or endive. It's wonderful accompanied by fruits like pears and citrus, as well as cucumbers, yellow and red bell peppers, celery, radishes and tomatoes. Watercress has a particular affinity for light, fruity dressings, like raspberry or citrus vinaigrettes, Asian-style dressings or balsamic vinegar-based dressings. Use it as an accent in salads where just a few greens are needed, or chop and include it in grain salads, pasta salads and potato salads to spice them up.

Watercress is highly nutritious, containing calcium, iron, and vitamins A and C, among other nutrients. It's also highly perishable, so select a lively looking bunch and keep it in a glass of water in the refrigerator, loosely covered with a plastic bag, for 2 or 3 days.

CARE OF GREENS

Purchasing

Choose lettuces and other greens that look fresh and crisp, avoiding any with bruised, wilted or decaying leaves.

As I've emphasized before, try to buy greens from a farm stand or farmers market if you can. What could be better than enjoying greens that have been picked on the same day you buy them? Lettuce or mesclun mixes purchased locally stay fresh longer—even as long as a week—when chilled and properly stored. All week long, you can have a steady supply of salad greens on hand.

Cleaning

Fill a salad spinner with cold water. Place the lettuce greens in the colander insert and swish them around, allowing any grit to fall to the bottom of the spinner bowl. Lift the colander insert from the water and check the bottom of the spinner bowl. If there is any sand or grit, discard the water and repeat the process. When the water is clear, lift colander, discard water, replace colander in spinner bowl and spin dry.

Spin-Drying

Dressings and vinaigrettes adhere best to very dry greens as any water left on the leaves will repel the oil in the vinaigrette. With my pull-cord spinner, I usually pull once or twice, then discard the bulk of the water. Then I pull the cord another 15 to 20 times, getting the greens really spinning to pull out as much water as possible.

Once thoroughly dried, place greens in the refrigerator—the cold will keep them crisp until ready for use.

Crisping Tip

If salad greens are slightly wilted when they arrive home from the store or market, place them in a salad spinner filled with very cold water and let them rest for 15 to 20 minutes. This replenishes the water that has evaporated from the leaves, reviving the greens and making them crisp again. Spin dry.

Storage

Until you wash greens, store them in a loosely closed plastic bag along with a dry paper towel or two to absorb the moisture that leads to decay. Once you have dried the greens, store them the same way. The greens will keep for several days or up to a week, depending on their initial freshness.

Lettuce or mesclun mixes purchased locally stay fresh longer—even as long as a week— when chilled and properly stored.

Clean Your Greens

There are few experiences as unpleasant as eating a gritty salad. Follow the directions on page 33 for the proper care and cleaning of greens.

Prepare Homemade Dressings

Fresh ingredients like leafy greens and vegetables taste best when tossed with a freshly made vinaigrette. I've tasted few bottled dressings that don't distract one's taste buds with odd or off flavors. Start by reading the basics, how to assemble a vinaigrette, or make one of the dozens of recipes for them offered in this book. Once you get the knack of balancing oil and vinegar or citrus in a vinaigrette, it only takes a minute or two to prepare one…and it's well worth it.

Use Extra-Virgin Olive Oil

Extra-virgin olive oil has the finest qualities of both flavor and aroma, and is the healthiest oil you can use for making salads. So-called "pure" or "light" olive oils mostly contain refined olive oil and some extra-virgin olive oil (unrefined)—as little as five percent. For all of the recipes in this book that require "olive oil" please use extra-virgin olive oil.

Tossing the Salad

How much dressing should be used? It depends on your own taste. The key to a perfect dressing is balance: you want enough dressing to flavor the lettuce and vegetables, but you don't want to drown them.

Tongs work nicely for tossing. Gently lift and mix the greens, up to 20 times or more, or until the dressing is evenly distributed. Start with a small amount of dressing, mix, taste, and add more if needed. You can also mix salads by hand. I keep a box of disposable plastic gloves nearby for this purpose—they're sold in restaurant or kitchen supply stores.

Tossing Tip

Have you ever made an inviting salad with colorful vegetables, only to toss it and end up with what looks like a bowl of lettuce with sunken vegetables hidden below? I have a good trick: keep the greens in one bowl; the vegetables in another. Add half of the vegetables to the greens and toss well with the dressing. Once tossed, add the rest of the vegetables and drizzle a little extra dressing on top.

Presentation

For vibrant color and texture in your salad, think contrast: mix dark, spicy greens like arugula and watercress with pale green lettuces like butterhead or Boston. Combine textures by including frisée, the frizzy member of the chicory family, endive sliced lengthwise or spiky mizuna.

Colorful vegetables play up salad greens, adding both interest and nutrition. Red radishes, white daikon radishes or sweet white jicama, cut into matchsticks or julienned, look beautiful with grapefruit or orange sections, strawberries or raspberries. Sliced yellow and red bell peppers are a bright touch for leafy greens, as are pale green celery and cucumber, razor-thin red onions or shaved red cabbage. Gorgeous radicchio leaves, sliced into ribbons, add a rich magenta hue to a sea of greens—from arugula to romaine.

If using cheese, always add it last: some Parmesan shaved with a vegetable peeler, mini feta cubes instead of crumbles. Herbs and edible flowers, when available, taste and look exquisite.

Experiment with wide, shallow bowls or long, large platters. These can really show off a salad with many ingredients and visual elements.

Salad Don'ts

Avoid using regular yellow onions or green bell peppers; their flavor is just too strong for use in salads. Use the sweeter red or yellow peppers instead. Red onions have a milder flavor that lend themselves well to salads. Skip using winter tomatoes, with the possible exception of ripe cherry tomatoes.

FIVE TERRIFIC SALAD TOOLS

Salad-making is easier—
and more enjoyable—
when you have these
simple tools close at
hand.

Salad Spinner

If you make a lot of salads, this inexpensive kitchen aid is essential. Its usefulness includes soaking, cleaning and drying all types of lettuce. Vinaigrettes adhere better to dry greens, and dry greens last longer in the refrigerator. In my own tests, the pull-cord spinner dries better and faster than push-button or other types. A favorite brand is Zyliss. Pull the spinner cord multiple times, not just once or twice, to remove as much moisture as possible. A mini salad spinner comes in very handy for cleaning fresh herbs; I'm surprised at how often I use both.

Tongs

Many chefs recommend tossing salad with your hands. Tongs, however, can do the trick without plunging your hands into wet, dressed salads. Gently lift and toss 15 to 20 times to evenly distribute the vinaigrette and just coat the salad.

Metal Bowls

Head to a restaurant supply store or browse the internet for several small, medium, and large stainless steel bowls. Because they're lightweight, metal bowls are easy to grasp, use and wash. You'll have light bowls in which to make vinaigrettes, larger bowls for tossing the salads, and bowls to hold prepped vegetables. Glass nesting bowls or colorful ceramic types are just too heavy for efficient, functional kitchen use.

A Few Good Whisks

Standard size whisks are generally too large and bulky for whipping up dressings in small- or medium-size bowls. Buy a variety of smaller whisks to have on hand.

Zester

The zest from grating the skins of lemons, limes and oranges adds another layer of flavor to all kinds of salads and dressings. The best tool for easily removing zest is the Microplane zester, available at kitchen supply stores. It has a long narrow rasp and plastic handle for easy handling. It's also a great tool for finely mincing ginger, shallots and garlic.

SERVES 4

BABY SPINACH AND STRAWBERRY SALAD

This is an elegant, colorful salad that is easy to make and is packed with vitamins. Feel free to substitute arugula for the spinach, or any other salad green you prefer. Both arugula and spinach have an affinity for fruity, citrusy flavors such as those of strawberry and orange. A good substitute for daikon radish would be jicama, a sweet, crunchy vegetable. Substitute about 1 or 2 cups raspberries or blackberries for the strawberries and you'll have an entirely different but equally delicious salad.

6 to 8 cups baby spinach or arugula, washed and dried

1 section (about 3 inches) daikon radish, peeled

2 oranges, peeled and cut into sections

10 to 12 strawberries, washed, hulled and sliced

ORANGE-RASPBERRY VINAIGRETTE

3 tablespoons raspberry, Moscatel or other light vinegar

1/3 cup fresh orange juice

2 teaspoons maple syrup or honey

1 teaspoon Dijon mustard

2 teaspoons finely minced shallots

6 tablespoons canola or olive oil

1/4 teaspoon kosher salt

1 Place the spinach in a salad bowl. Holding a very sharp knife at a 45-degree angle, cut the daikon radish into the thinnest slices you can make, then cut each slice into thin matchsticks. Add to the spinach.

2 To make the dressing, in a bowl, whisk together the vinegar, juice, maple syrup, mustard, shallots, oil and salt. Just before serving, drizzle the vinaigrette over the salad; mix well. Add orange sections and sliced strawberries, and drizzle a little more vinaigrette over all. Serve immediately.

RASPBERRY VINEGARS The best raspberry vinegar is made with real raspberries, and because it's a star ingredient in the vinaigrette for this salad, it's worth seeking out. My favorite is the Queen of Hearts raspberry vinegar available from a sustainable farm in New Hampshire. It combines fresh raspberries, vinegar and a touch of wildflower honey. Check out www.cheshiregarden.com.

SERVES 4

MIXED GREEN SALAD WITH ROASTED FIGS AND PISTACHIOS

When it's fig season, from May to June and August to September, use figs as a "garnish" for tender, leafy green salads. Sweet, ripe figs pair beautifully with balsamic or port wine vinegar, gorgonzola or goat cheese and nuts, so that's how I usually compose this salad. You can serve the figs fresh, cut into quarters, or cut in half and roasted, as in this recipe.

6 fresh ripe Black Mission figs, halved

1 tablespoon sugar

6 to 8 cups arugula or mixed baby greens, washed and dried

4 ounces crumbled goat cheese

1/4 cup shelled pistachio nuts (preferably unsalted)

BALSAMIC VINAIGRETTE

5 to 6 tablespoons olive oil

2 tablespoons balsamic or port wine vinegar

Salt and pepper

1 Preheat the oven to 350°. Place the sugar on a small plate and dip the cut sides of the figs into it. Heat an oven-proof skillet over medium to medium-high heat and coat with olive oil. Place figs in the hot pan cut-side down and cook until they're lightly browned, about 5 or 6 minutes. Remove skillet from the heat and turn figs cut side up. A short time before serving, place the skillet with the figs into the oven and roast until they're warm and softened, 15 to 20 minutes.

2 To make the dressing, in a small bowl, whisk together the oil and vinegar. Season with salt and pepper.

3 This salad can be plated individually or on a serving platter. Place the greens in a bowl and dress with just enough vinaigrette to coat them. Toss well until vinaigrette is evenly distributed. Place greens on plates or on a platter and top with the figs. Garnish the salad with goat cheese and pistachio nuts.

PAIRING FIGS When I need some new ideas, I often turn to *Culinary Artistry* by Karen Page and Andrew Dorenburg. They've compiled a directory of ingredients with notes on what pairs well with a number of key ingredients. They call this section "Food Matches Made in Heaven." Here are a few favorable fig combinations to help spark more ideas for salads that include this delicious fruit: almonds, brown sugar, caramel, chocolate, cinnamon, cream, ginger, honey, lemon, lavender, mint, orange, Parma ham, peaches, pears, prosciutto, raspberries, rosemary, strawberries and red wine.

LEAFY GREEN AND VEGETABLE SALAD WITH LEMON-TAHINI DRESSING

Fresh-tasting Lemon-Tahini Dressing can be used with a variety of leafy greens and vegetable combinations. Here, it's red leaf lettuce with shredded carrot, cucumber, red onion and a mild-tasting seaweed called arame, which lends unexpected flavor and nutrition. Arame can often be found in the Asian section of your supermarket.

1 head red leaf lettuce or other greens (6 to 8 cups), washed and dried
1 cup finely shredded red cabbage
1/4 red onion, sliced razor thin
1 cucumber, peeled, quartered and sliced
1/4 cup dried arame seaweed
1 large carrot, julienned
Toasted sunflower or sesame seeds, for garnish

LEMON-TAHINI DRESSING
2 tablespoons fresh lemon juice
1 tablespoon tahini
2 teaspoons soy sauce
1/2 teaspoon finely minced garlic
1/4 cup olive oil
1 tablespoon minced fresh parsley
Salt and pepper

1 In a large bowl, combine the lettuce, cabbage, red onion and cucumber.

2 Place the arame in a small bowl and cover with boiling water. Set aside until water is cool; drain.

3 To make the dressing, whisk together the lemon juice, tahini, soy sauce, garlic, oil, parsley, salt and pepper; set aside.

4 Just before serving, dress the salad with desired amount of dressing. Top with shredded carrots and arame. Drizzle a little more dressing over all and garnish with sunflower or sesame seeds.

ARUGULA AND AVOCADO SALAD WITH SHAVED PARMESAN

This is a simple, classic combination of arugula and shaved Parmesan cheese with a lemony dressing. With such a simple salad, it's nice to use the more flavorful imported aged Parmigiano Reggiano. You can vary this salad with sliced cucumber or tomato wedges, homemade croutons, sliced endive or radicchio.

2 bunches arugula, washed and dried (about 6 cups)
1 avocado, sliced
Shaved Parmigiano Reggiano, to taste

LEMON DRESSING
2 tablespoons fresh lemon juice
1 medium clove garlic, finely minced
4 to 5 tablespoons olive oil
Salt and ground pepper

1 To make the dressing, in a small bowl, combine the lemon juice and garlic. Slowly whisk in olive oil until the mixture is creamy. Season with salt and pepper.

2 Place arugula in a serving bowl and add dressing to taste. Mix well. Top with avocado slices, drizzle a bit more dressing over them and season with a pinch of salt. Using a vegetable peeler, shave slivers of Parmesan over the top.

SERVES 2

FARMERS MARKET SALAD

When I bring home a pile of vegetables from the local farmers market I like to make this Cobb-like salad for my husband and myself. For protein, I use leftover fish, chicken, hard-boiled eggs or cheese—whatever's on hand. Almost any homemade dressing will do for this combo—Herb Vinaigrette, Basil Balsamic, Creamy Lemon, Italian, Greek Herb, Creamy Ranch or just a simple oil and vinegar mix.

3 cups lettuce greens, rinsed and dried
1 tomato, cut into wedges
1 small cucumber, peeled, cut in half lengthwise and sliced
2 radishes, thinly sliced and quartered
1/2 thick carrot, peeled and cut into matchsticks
1/4 small red onion, very thinly sliced
2 hard boiled eggs, quartered
1 cup croutons (optional)
1/4 cup crumbled goat or feta cheese (optional)

VINAIGRETTE
1 tablespoon red wine vinegar
1 teaspoon fresh lemon juice
1/2 teaspoon dried oregano
1/4 teaspoon finely minced garlic
4 tablespoons olive oil
Salt and pepper

1 In a large bowl, combine the lettuce, tomato, cucumber, radish, carrot and red onion.

2 To make the dressing, in a small bowl, whisk together the vinegar, lemon juice, oregano and garlic, then whisk in the oil. Season with salt and pepper.

3 Add enough dressing to coat the salad and toss to combine. Divide salad between two plates or large shallow bowls. Garnish with eggs or other protein source of your choice, croutons and cheese, if desired.

HARD-BOILING EGGS Place **2** eggs in a medium saucepan and fill with enough cold water to cover the eggs by **2** inches. Bring to a boil. When the water begins to boil, turn off the heat and let eggs remain in pan, covered, for **10** minutes. Remove the eggs and run them under cold water or place in a bowl of cold water before removing the shells.

BABY GREEN SALAD WITH BLUEBERRIES, MELON AND STRAWBERRIES

A salad with blueberries, strawberries and melon is striking and delicious. It's also full of the antioxidant properties a healthy body craves. This trio works well with baby greens, baby spinach, arugula or watercress. Sometimes I like to add diced cucumber.

6 cups baby lettuce greens or arugula, washed and dried

1 cup blueberries

1 cup honeydew melon, diced

1 cup hulled and sliced strawberries

5 basil or mint leaves, finely slivered (optional)

RASPBERRY VINAIGRETTE

1 tablespoon raspberry vinegar

2 tablespoons fresh tangerine juice or orange juice

1/2 teaspoon honey

2 tablespoons olive oil

Salt

1 To make the dressing, in a small bowl, whisk together the vinegar, juice, honey and oil; season with salt.

2 Place the greens in a large bowl and add enough dressing to lightly coat them. Toss well. Divide the greens among 4 plates or arrange on a large serving platter. Scatter the blueberries, honeydew and strawberries over the salad. Drizzle a little more dressing over the fruit and garnish with slivered fresh basil or mint, cut just before serving.

VARIATION If you don't have raspberry vinegar on hand, try this subtle combination: in a small bowl, whisk 1 tablespoon balsamic vinegar, 1 tablespoon fresh lime juice, 1/2 teaspoon honey, 4 tablespoons olive oil and salt and pepper to taste.

SERVES 4 TO 6

CITRUS SALAD WITH CHAMPAGNE VINAIGRETTE

This is another of my favorite cold-weather salads—it's light and refreshing, with juicy sections of orange and pink grapefruit. Any salad green can be used, but the more peppery greens like arugula, watercress, and frisée have a particular affinity for sweet citrus. A mix of arugula, butterhead lettuce and radicchio makes a colorful, festive salad for entertaining. The crunch in the salad comes from slivers of daikon radish, which looks like a giant white carrot. If daikon is unavailable, substitute 3 to 4 red radishes or julienned jicama.

2 pink grapefruits, peeled and cut into sections

3 naval oranges, peeled and cut into sections

1 section (about 3 inches) daikon radish, peeled and cut into matchsticks (about 1/2 cup)

6 to 8 cups lettuce (a single variety or a mix of greens) washed and dried

CHAMPAGNE VINAIGRETTE

1/3 cup leftover juice from oranges and grapefruit

2 tablespoons Champagne or rice vinegar

1 teaspoon finely minced shallot

5 tablespoons olive oil

2 pinches salt

1 Reserve the pulpy membrane from the grapefruit and oranges for the vinaigrette and squeeze their excess juices into a small bowl.

2 Make the vinaigrette by mixing the reserved citrus juice, vinegar and shallot together in a small bowl. Whisk in the oil and season with salt.

3 Mix the daikon radish and lettuce, then add just enough dressing to coat the salad. (You may have some dressing left over.) Transfer salad to a serving bowl and top with citrus sections.

MIXED GREEN SALAD WITH LEMON-WALNUT DRESSING

Introducing apples and walnuts to a mix of textured lettuces makes an intriguing fall/winter salad—one that's perfect for entertaining. At other times of the year, substitute fruits that are in season: peaches, raspberries, blackberries, pears or citrus. The dressing deliciously handles them all. If you'd like to enjoy these interesting greens solo, omit the fruit altogether.

1/3 cup walnuts
1 small head Boston or butterhead lettuce, or 3 cups mixed greens, washed and dried
1 cup slivered radicchio
1 cup frisée (if available), washed, dried and torn into bite-size pieces
1 endive, cored and cut lengthwise into slivers
1 crisp apple, cut into quarters and cored
Fresh lemon juice
4 ounces goat cheese, crumbled

LEMON-WALNUT DRESSING
1/3 cup walnuts
2 tablespoons fresh lemon juice
1/2 teaspoon dry mustard
1 & 1/2 teaspoons honey or maple syrup
3 tablespoons olive oil
Salt and pepper

1 To toast the walnuts for both the salad and the dressing, preheat the oven to 350°. Place nuts on a baking sheet and roast for 7 to 9 minutes. Remove from oven and let cool. Rub the cooled nuts with your hands or place in a cotton towel to remove as much brown skin as possible. Roughly chop the walnuts and set aside.

2 Combine the lettuce, radicchio, frisée and endive in a salad bowl or on a serving platter. Slice each apple quarter as thinly as possible; sprinkle with a few drops of lemon juice to prevent discoloring. Add apple slices to the salad and top with crumbled goat cheese and chopped walnuts.

3 To make the dressing, place 1/3 cup toasted walnuts in a blender or food processor and process until they are finely chopped. Add 2 tablespoons water, lemon juice, mustard, honey or maple syrup, oil, and salt and pepper; blend until dressing is creamy (if it's too thick to pour, thin it out by whisking or blending in up to 3 teaspoons of water, a teaspoon at a time). Serve the dressing on the side.

APPLE, POMEGRANATE AND ARUGULA SALAD WITH APPLE CIDER-HONEY VINAIGRETTE

A great salad for autumn, simply made with leafy greens, slivers of apple and juicy red pomegranate seeds.

1 crisp apple
Fresh lemon juice
6 to 7 cups arugula, washed and dried,
stems removed
1/4 cup pomegranate seeds, page 24
1/4 cup toasted sliced almonds
Goat cheese, crumbled

APPLE CIDER-HONEY VINAIGRETTE
2 tablespoons apple cider vinegar
1 & 1/2 teaspoons honey
6 tablespoons olive oil
2 pinches salt

1 Wash the apple and cut into quarters, leaving the peel intact. With a paring knife or corer, remove the core from two of the quarters and slice them as thinly as possible. Save the remaining two quarters for a healthful snack. Place the slices in a bowl and drizzle with a little lemon juice to keep them from discoloring.

2 In a small bowl, make the vinaigrette by whisking together the vinegar, honey, olive oil and salt.

3 Just before serving, toss the arugula and apples with just enough dressing to coat the leaves. Divide salad among four plates. Sprinkle each serving with about 1 tablespoon of pomegranate seeds, or more to taste. Top with the toasted sliced almonds and crumbled goat cheese.

GREEK SALAD

A real classic, this is still one of the most refreshing salads around, and one that pairs well with many main courses. During winter or spring, use the more flavorful cherry tomatoes that are available.

1 head romaine lettuce, washed and dried (4 to 6 cups)

2 medium cucumbers, peeled, seeded and cut into 1/2-inch dice

3 tomatoes, cut into wedges, or 1/2 pound cherry tomatoes, halved

1/2 small red onion, sliced paper-thin

1/2 pound feta cheese, crumbled

1/2 cup pitted kalamata olives, quartered lengthwise

GREEK DRESSING

2 tablespoons red wine vinegar

1 tablespoon fresh lemon juice

1 clove garlic, finely minced

1 & 1/2 teaspoons dried oregano

1/2 cup olive oil

Salt and pepper

1 Trim the romaine and chop it into bite-size pieces. Place the lettuce in a large bowl and combine with the cucumbers, tomatoes and red onion.

2 To make the dressing, in a small bowl, combine the vinegar, lemon juice, garlic and oregano. Add the oil in a steady stream, whisking constantly. Generously season with salt and pepper.

3 Just before serving, whisk the dressing again and add enough to the salad to thoroughly coat the ingredients. Reserve leftover dressing for another salad. Top with feta cheese and olives.

SERVES 4

LEAFY GREEN SALAD WITH GRILLED TOFU

Tofu marinated in lemon and herbs, then grilled, adds delicious protein to this big salad. Tangy Lemon-Tahini Dressing pulls it all together. The entire dish is easy to assemble—don't be put off by the lengthy list of ingredients, most of which are used for the marinade and dressing.

TOFU MARINADE

1 pound extra-firm tofu
1/4 cup fresh lemon juice
1/4 cup olive oil, plus more for the pan
1 tablespoon soy sauce
2 cloves garlic, finely minced
2 tablespoons chopped, mixed fresh herbs, such as parsley, chives, basil or thyme

SALAD

6 cups leafy lettuce greens, washed and dried
1 tomato, cut into small wedges
1 cucumber, peeled, quartered and sliced
1/2 thick carrot, peeled and cut into matchsticks
4 radishes, thinly sliced and quartered
Basil leaves and/or chopped chives, for garnish (optional)

1 Wrap the tofu in a clean kitchen towel or in several layers of paper towels, and allow it to rest for at least 10 minutes (the towels absorb moisture from the tofu). Cut tofu into 1-inch chunks—you should have about 24 pieces.

2 To make the marinade, in a large bowl, combine the lemon juice, oil, soy sauce, garlic and herbs. Add the tofu and marinate the mixture for at least 1 hour.

3 Heat a stovetop grill pan over medium-high heat. (If you don't own a stovetop grill pan, you can sear the tofu in a large, heavy skillet, such as a cast iron pan. You can also broil it.) If grilling the tofu, threading the cubes onto skewers makes it easier. (If using wood skewers, soak them in water for 30 minutes before using.) Reserve the marinade. Brush the grill pan with oil and grill the tofu for a total of about 10 to 12 minutes, until each piece is golden on all sides. If using a skillet, sauté over medium-high heat until golden on all sides. Do not allow pieces to burn. When the tofu is cooked, spoon a tablespoon or two of the marinade over it for extra flavor. Because tofu is not a raw product you can do this safely.

4 To assemble the salad, place the salad greens in a large, wide bowl or on a serving platter. Top with the tomato, cucumber, carrot and radishes. Remove tofu from skewers and place the pieces on top of the salad. Just before serving, tear the basil leaves and scatter the pieces, and/or the chives, over all.

5 To make the dressing, in a small bowl, whisk together the lemon juice, tahini, soy sauce, garlic, oil, parsley, salt and pepper. Serve the dressing on the side.

LEMON-TAHINI DRESSING
2 tablespoons fresh lemon juice
1 tablespoon tahini
2 teaspoons soy sauce
1/2 teaspoon minced garlic
1/4 cup olive oil
1 tablespoon minced fresh parsley
Salt and pepper

SERVES 4

ROASTED APRICOT AND ARUGULA SALAD WITH GORGONZOLA

Slightly sweet roasted apricots, creamy gorgonzola (a cow's milk blue cheese from northern Italy) and peppery arugula create a simple but standout salad. Try adding toasted nuts such as hazelnuts, sliced almonds or pine nuts—I'll let you decide.

4 apricots, halved, pits removed
Olive oil
6 to 8 cups baby arugula, washed and dried
1 cup thinly sliced radicchio
1/2 cup crumbled gorgonzola cheese

BALSAMIC VINAIGRETTE
2 tablespoons balsamic vinegar
5 tablespoons olive oil
Salt and pepper

1 Preheat the oven to 350°. Brush apricots on both sides with olive oil and place them flesh side up on a rimmed baking sheet lined with parchment paper. Roast until apricots are cooked and slightly softened but not collapsed, about 15 to 18 minutes. Set aside to cool slightly.

2 To make the dressing, in a small bowl, whisk together the vinegar and oil; season with salt and pepper.

3 In a large bowl, toss the arugula and radicchio with just enough dressing to coat the leaves. Divide salad among four individual plates and top each serving with two apricot halves. Top with crumbled gorgonzola. Drizzle a bit more dressing over the salad.

VARIATION If you can't find fresh apricots, you can use 6 to 8 soft and plump dried apricots, thinly sliced. Roasted or grilled peaches would also make a fine substitute.

SHERRY VINEGAR O Olive Oil Co. makes a sherry vinegar with a touch of apricot wine added to soften the vinegar's acidity. Because of its hint of sweet fruit, it would pair nicely with this salad, and could be substituted for the balsamic vinegar. Whisk 2 tablespoons O Sherry Apricot Vinegar with 6 tablespoons olive oil.

SERVES 2 TO 4

THAI MELON SALAD

Spicy, sweet and sour flavors meld wonderfully in Rachel Travers's triple melon mix. A Boston-based food writer and friend, Rachel uses cantaloupe, honeydew and watermelon, letting the juices from each mingle with the other ingredients. Use as much or as little of each variety of melon as you like. This is a dish that's simple to make and ultra refreshing.

About 3 cups of 3 varieties of melon, cut into 1/2-inch dice
Pinch of cayenne pepper
Juice of 1/2 lime
Chopped fresh cilantro, for garnish
Chopped unsalted dry-roasted peanuts, for garnish

1 In a large bowl, combine the diced melons. Add a small pinch of cayenne and lime juice to taste.

2 Top with the chopped cilantro and peanuts.

ARUGULA AND RADICCHIO SALAD WITH ORANGES, WALNUTS AND GOAT CHEESE

During the cold winter months, I think of citrus as a refreshing addition to salads because they nicely balance the heartier winter foods. Like tomatoes in the summer, orange or grapefruit sections perk up salads with a touch of sweet acidity and juiciness. A little tangy cheese and toasted nuts help round out the flavors.

6 cups baby arugula, butterhead lettuce or romaine, washed and dried

1 small head radicchio cut into quarters, cored and thinly sliced (about 2 cups)

2 navel oranges, peeled and cut into sections

1/3 cup crumbled goat cheese or blue cheese

1/3 cup walnuts, toasted and chopped

BALSAMIC VINAIGRETTE
3 tablespoons balsamic vinegar

1 teaspoon Dijon mustard

1 to 2 teaspoons maple syrup

2 teaspoons minced shallot

1/2 cup olive oil

Salt and pepper

1 Chop or tear the lettuces into bite-size pieces. If desired, soak radicchio in a bowl of cold water for 10 minutes to remove some of its bitterness. Drain and dry well.

2 To make the dressing, in a small bowl, whisk together the vinegar, mustard, maple syrup and shallot. Whisk in oil until mixture is creamy; add salt and pepper to taste. Just before serving, place the lettuces and radicchio in a wide shallow serving bowl. Add just enough dressing to coat the leaves; mix well. Reserve leftover dressing for another salad. Top with the orange sections, cheese and toasted walnuts.

VARIATION This salad is also delicious with Reduced Orange Vinaigrette, page 248.

BIBB, WATERCRESS AND ENDIVE SALAD WITH PEARS, WALNUTS AND POMEGRANATE SEEDS

I created this recipe for my friend Sharon Eber, who is partial to pear salads in the fall and wanted to try a new one for the holidays. The combination of autumn pears and seasonal pomegranate seeds with leafy greens gives each mouthful a burst of refreshing flavor. Crisp, juicy Asian pears are a unique addition, if available. Whichever variety of pear you use, the fruit is best sliced at the last minute to prevent discoloration.

1 pomegranate

**1 bunch watercress, rinsed and dried, large
   stems removed, roughly chopped**

**2 heads bibb or Boston lettuce, rinsed and
   dried, torn into pieces**

**2 endives, cored and thinly sliced
   lengthwise**

**1 Asian pear, cored and cut into very thin
   slices, or 2 firm but ripe pears, cored and
   thinly sliced**

1/2 cup walnuts, toasted and chopped

**4 ounces gorgonzola or blue cheese,
   crumbled**

BASIC VINAIGRETTE

2 tablespoons vinegar (Champagne,
   balsamic, or red wine vinegar)

6 tablespoons olive oil

Salt and pepper

RASPBERRY VINAIGRETTE

3 tablespoons raspberry vinegar

4 tablespoons fresh orange juice

1 teaspoon maple syrup, honey or sugar

1 tablespoon chopped shallot or red onion

6 tablespoons canola or olive oil, or a
   blend of both

1/4 teaspoon kosher salt

1 Open the pomegranate as described on page 24 and set aside about 1/2 cup of the seeds.

2 In a large bowl, combine the watercress, lettuce and endives. Prepare the vinaigrette of your choice by whisking the ingredients; add salt and pepper to taste.

3 Just before serving, add just enough dressing to coat the greens and toss well. Place salad on a large shallow serving platter. Top the greens with sliced pears and pomegranate seeds, and drizzle with a little more dressing over all. Top with walnuts and cheese.

SERVES 4

ROASTED PEAR-HONEY SALAD WITH BABY GREENS

Just as pears love blue cheese, honey does too—its sweet touch tames the blue cheese bite. When added to greens, the trio makes for an elegant salad. Experiment with several blue cheeses to discover which ones you like best. If you live in New England, try the Great Hill Blue Cheese, made in Massachusetts and sold at Whole Foods Markets.

2 pears, peeled, halved and cored

2 teaspoons honey

6 to 8 cups mixed baby greens, washed and dried

4 ounces blue cheese, crumbled

1/3 cup walnuts or hazelnuts, toasted and chopped

BALSAMIC VINAIGRETTE

2 tablespoons balsamic vinegar

1 teaspoon finely minced shallot

4 to 6 tablespoons olive oil

Salt and pepper

1 Preheat the oven to 375°. Line a baking sheet with parchment paper. Brush the pears with a little oil, place pears on the prepared baking sheet cut sides down, and bake for 20 to 25 minutes. The pears should be browned on the bottom and easily pierced with a fork, but not meltingly soft. When the pears are browned, turn them over and drizzle each with 1/2 teaspoon of honey, letting most of it pool in the scooped-out core. Bake for an additional 5 minutes. (Pears can be made ahead the same day, but do not refrigerate them.)

2 To make the vinaigrette, in a small bowl combine the vinegar and shallot, then whisk in the oil. Season with salt and pepper.

3 Place salad greens in a medium bowl and toss with just enough dressing to coat the leaves. Mix well. Divide the salad among 4 plates; top each serving with a pear half and top with blue cheese and nuts.

BALSAMIC VINEGAR When you want to wow your family or friends, use your best balsamic vinegar. If you want to splurge, try this bottle I've found at Whole Foods Market: Villa Manodori Aceto Balsamico di Modena ($28). It makes the best salads imaginable. The sweeter and more aged the vinegar, the less oil you will need.

ARUGULA AND ORANGE SALAD WITH FIG-TANGERINE DRESSING

The sweetness of fig jam and citrus combined with peppery arugula and slightly salty blue cheese is an unbeatable combination—very tasty and refreshing. It is the creation of Michael Scott, manager of the cheese department for the Newtonville, Massachusetts, Whole Foods Market.

6 to 7 cups baby arugula, washed and dried
Orange segments from 2 navel oranges, or 1 can (11 ounces) mandarin oranges
1/4 cup chopped toasted walnuts
Blue cheese, crumbled, for garnish

FIG-TANGERINE DRESSING
3 tablespoons prepared fig jam or spread such as Dalmatia or Adriatic brand
4 tablespoons fresh tangerine juice
1/4 teaspoon fresh lemon juice
Pinch of salt

1 Place the arugula in a serving dish and top with orange sections. Top with the walnuts and blue cheese.

2 To make the dressing, in a small bowl, whisk together fig jam, tangerine juice and lemon juice until smooth; season with a pinch of salt. Drizzle a generous amount of dressing over the salad.

SERVES 4

LEAFY GREEN SALAD WITH LEMON-BASIL GOAT CHEESE

In this salad, I've combined the salad greens with a goat cheese appetizer that a friend, Hilary Noyes-Keene, once brought to a party. The goat cheese was topped with lemon zest, garlic and fresh herbs. Farm-fresh greens or arugula will taste best here. Serve this salad with a sliced, freshly baked baguette or a loaf of country-style bread for spreading the cheese.

6 to 8 ounces of your favorite goat cheese

1 teaspoon grated lemon zest

1/2 teaspoon finely minced garlic

2 tablespoons olive oil

Salt and pepper

6 to 8 cups arugula or mixed baby greens, washed and dried

4 to 6 fresh basil leaves

1 baguette or loaf of country-style bread, sliced

BALSAMIC VINAIGRETTE
2 tablespoons balsamic vinegar
5 to 6 tablespoons olive oil
Salt and pepper

1 Using either a mold or your hands, gently form the goat cheese into 4 disks measuring approximately 2-inches wide by 1/3- to 1/2-inch thick. In a small bowl, mix the lemon zest, garlic, oil and pinch of salt. Place the rounds of cheese on a plate, season with freshly ground pepper and evenly pour the mixture over them. Cover plate and refrigerate until ready to serve.

2 To make the dressing, in a small bowl, whisk together the balsamic vinegar and oil; season with salt and pepper.

3 Place arugula or greens in a bowl and add the desired amount of dressing; mix well. Divide the greens among 4 salad plates. Top each serving with a disk of the goat cheese, including the mixture they marinated in. Sliver the basil and sprinkle over the goat cheese. Place a few slices of baguette on each plate.

SERVES 4

PEA SHOOTS AND EDAMAME

Tender, delicate-tasting pea shoots make a cool salad your friends will love. Because they are highly perishable, pea shoots will wilt quickly once they're dressed, so do so at the table just before serving. Serve this salad as a first course. If pea shoots are unavailable, use delicate, nutty-tasting mâche, watercress, baby spinach or baby arugula.

2/3 cup edamame beans (fresh or frozen)
1 large celery stalk, peeled
2 radishes, trimmed
4 to 6 cups pea shoot greens

ASIAN VINAIGRETTE
1 tablespoon rice vinegar
2 tablespoons fresh lemon juice or lime juice
1 teaspoon finely minced fresh ginger
1 tablespoon honey
1 tablespoon soy sauce
3 tablespoons canola or grapeseed oil
2 teaspoons dark sesame oil

CHAMPAGNE VINAIGRETTE
1/4 cup fresh orange or grapefruit juice
2 tablespoons Champagne vinegar
1 teaspoon finely minced shallot
5 tablespoons olive oil
2 pinches of kosher salt

1 Bring a small saucepan of salted water to a boil. Add the edamame beans and cook, uncovered, over medium-high heat for 3 to 4 minutes until tender. Drain edamame in a colander and run them under cold water until cool.

2 Slice the celery stalk in half lengthwise, then, holding your knife on the diagonal slice it crosswise into the thinnest slices possible. Cut the radish into thin slices, then cut each slice into matchsticks. In a small bowl, mix edamame, celery and radishes; set aside.

3 Just before serving, place pea shoots in a serving bowl. Choose whichever vinaigrette you're in the mood for and whisk dressing ingredients together in a bowl. Dress the salad with just enough vinaigrette to coat the greens, tossing gently. Add some dressing to the vegetables, toss to coat, then arrange them on top of the salad. Serve immediately. Reserve leftover dressing for another salad.

EDAMAME Edamame, or fresh soybeans, come in fuzzy, light green pods. The bean inside is light green and smooth, and has an appealing, nutty flavor. Nutritionally, edamame beans are a complete protein with calcium, iron, zinc, folate, vitamins C and A, fiber and minimal fat content. Fresh edamame beans directly purchased from a farmers market have a lot of flavor, but the frozen versions taste pretty good and are conveniently already shelled.

ROMAINE AND CUCUMBER CAESAR SALAD

If you haven't prepared a homemade Caesar salad dressing or homemade croutons in a while, give them a try again—they make the salad so special. You can leave out the eggs, if desired; the dressing will still be good but not as creamy. (Try adding a little mayonnaise in place of the eggs for a creamier texture.) This recipe makes more dressing than necessary, so if you need to increase the salad to serve more people, it's no problem.

2 cups Italian or sourdough bread cut into 1/2-inch cubes
1 teaspoon finely minced garlic
4 teaspoons olive oil
Salt and pepper
1 head romaine lettuce (6 to 8 cups), washed and dried
1 cucumber, peeled, seeded and thinly sliced
1/4 cup grated Parmigiano Reggiano cheese, or more to taste

LEMON DRESSING
1 egg yolk
3 anchovy fillets
1/2 teaspoon minced garlic
1 teaspoon Dijon mustard
3 tablespoons fresh lemon juice
1/2 cup olive oil
Salt and pepper

1 To make croutons, preheat the oven to 350°. In a medium bowl, mix the bread cubes and the garlic. Drizzle olive oil over the bread and toss with salt and pepper. Place on a baking sheet; bake for 10 to 12 minutes or until croutons are lightly crisp, but still chewy inside.

2 To make the dressing, place the egg yolks, anchovies, garlic, mustard and lemon juice in the bowl of a food processor; process thoroughly. Keep the processor running and add the oil until dressing is creamy. Add salt and pepper to taste. If you don't own a food processor, mince the anchovy fillets and place in a small bowl. Whisk in the egg yolks, garlic, mustard and lemon juice. Add the olive oil in a thin, steady stream, whisking constantly, until the dressing is creamy. Season with salt and pepper.

3 Trim the romaine and chop or tear the leaves into bite-size pieces. Place romaine and cucumber in a large bowl and add just enough dressing to coat the greens. Mix well. Sprinkle with cheese and top with garlic croutons.

VARIATIONS I also like to add other vegetables to my salad with Caesar dressing, including avocado, tomato or sliced red onion. Make a Chicken Caesar Salad by topping greens with strips of grilled chicken, or try adding poached shrimp for a light meal. Substitute some different greens, such as baby greens, arugula or watercress for the romaine.

MIXED GREENS AND ROASTED PEAR SALAD

Roasting pears in the oven gives them a delicious, caramelized flavor that transforms an ordinary salad into something special. I like Anjou pears, slightly ripened to the point at which my finger makes a dent when the fruit is pressed, but that are not too soft. Bake the pears until they are golden brown on the bottom (if they are not browning, turn up the heat as they bake, if they bake too fast, quickly turn them over).

3 pears, peeled, halved and cored
Olive oil
1 small head red leaf or bibb lettuce, washed and dried
1 bunch arugula, large stems removed, washed and dried
1/2 small red onion, thinly sliced
4 ounces goat cheese or blue cheese, crumbled
1/3 cup chopped, toasted walnuts

PEAR VINAIGRETTE
1/2 roasted pear
1/4 cup olive oil
1/4 cup apple or pear juice
2 tablespoons red wine, sherry or apple cider vinegar
1 teaspoon fresh lemon juice
Salt and pepper

1 Preheat the oven to 375°. Brush the pears with a little olive oil, place them on a baking sheet cut sides down, and bake for 20 to 25 minutes. The pears should be browned on the bottom and easily pierced with a fork. Set aside to cool. Reserve half of one pear for the dressing.

2 In a large bowl, mix the lettuce, arugula and red onion.

3 To make the vinaigrette, place the reserved roasted pear half, oil, apple or pear juice, vinegar, lemon juice, and salt and pepper in a food processor or blender. Process until mixture is pureed. Add a little more oil or juice to thin the mixture, if necessary. Add enough dressing to coat the salad; mix well, then divide the salad among individual plates. Top each serving with a roasted pear half and sprinkle goat or blue cheese over all. Top with toasted walnuts.

SERVES 4

ARUGULA, CELERY AND DATE SALAD WITH WHITE BALSAMIC VINAIGRETTE

In her book *Cooking School Secrets for Real World Cooks*, hometown friend Linda Carucci combines plump sweet dates with cool, crunchy celery and a garnish of walnuts and feta cheese. Here, the salad undergoes some subtle changes, most notably with the addition of peppery arugula. Use dried dates that are soft and plump, not shriveled or crystallized.

5 to 6 cups baby arugula, washed and dried

3 large celery stalks, peeled and thinly sliced on the diagonal

1/4 cup chopped celery leaves (optional)

6 to 8 large dried pitted Medjool dates, cut into strips

1/2 cup walnuts, toasted and chopped

4 ounces feta cheese, crumbled

WHITE BALSAMIC VINAIGRETTE
4 teaspoons white balsamic vinegar
Salt and pepper
3 tablespoons olive oil

1 In a bowl or on a serving platter combine the arugula, celery and celery leaves.

2 To make the dressing, in a small bowl, combine the vinegar, salt and a few grinds of pepper; whisk in the olive oil.

3 Just before serving, pour dressing over the salad and toss to combine. Top with dates, walnuts and feta cheese.

VEGETABLE LOVERS SALAD

What makes this salad a little different is the size of the vegetables—they are all cut into a fine, uniform dice so that they appear like jewels on the lettuce. Every mouthful contains a cache of tiny gems.

1 head loose leaf, butterhead or romaine lettuce, washed and dried

1 celery stalk, cut into 1/4-inch dice

1/2 cucumber, peeled, seeded and cut into 1/4-inch dice

1 carrot, peeled and cut into 1/4-inch dice

1/2 red or yellow bell pepper, cored and cut into 1/4-inch dice

1/4 red onion, cut into 1/4-inch dice

BALSAMIC VINAIGRETTE

3 tablespoons balsamic vinegar

1 teaspoon Dijon mustard

2 teaspoons maple syrup

2 teaspoons minced shallot

1/2 cup olive oil

Salt and pepper

1 Cut or tear the lettuce into bite-size pieces. Place lettuce in a large shallow bowl or on a serving platter. In another bowl, set the diced vegetables aside.

2 To make the dressing, in a separate small bowl, whisk together the vinegar, mustard, maple syrup and shallot. Add the oil in a thin, steady stream, whisking constantly. Add salt and pepper to taste. Add just enough vinaigrette to coat the lettuce. Reserve leftover dressing for another salad. When the salad is dressed, scatter the vegetables over the top and drizzle them with a little more dressing.

VARIATION This salad is also good with Basil-Balsamic Vinaigrette on page 244.

CHICKEN SALAD EVERY WAY

CHICKEN SALAD EVERY WAY

When I was growing up, my family had one recipe each for chicken, pasta, and potato salad. They were all adequate, but having them year after year became a little boring. My sister still makes these recipes, and my bet is that others also make the same recipes again and again. One of my prime motivations in writing this book was to offer more choices—lots of choices—especially for chicken salads.

To start with, the chicken in chicken salads can be grilled, sautéed or roasted, not just poached and mixed with mayonnaise. Chicken salads can also reflect ethnic influences and make use of the interesting produce we see in stores today. Vegetables and fruits enhance many salads, including chicken salads, and I like to take full advantage of them for good taste and good health.

Now when I think about making a chicken salad, I choose one that best suits the occasion. For a break from the ordinary, I might make an Asian-style salad, such as the Roasted Chinese Chicken with Snow Peas and Water Chestnuts (page 92)—crunchy, fresh and spicy. Or the Chicken Salad with Bok Choy, Celery and Peanut-Ginger Vinaigrette (page 75), bursting veggies and coated with a light, luscious peanut sauce.

For family gatherings, my choice of salad requires that I get my dad's approval and consider the kids' tastes plus everyone in between. For such occasions, I developed the Grilled Chicken Salad with Red and Yellow Peppers and Honey-Dijon Vinaigrette (page 83). Slices of grilled chicken mingle with leafy greens, slivered celery, red onion and colorful peppers. I serve it outside at the picnic table along with a summer tomato and fresh mozzarella pasta salad, and everyone's happy. The Provençal Chicken Salad (page 91) also looks wonderful when presented on a platter with grilled chicken, sun-dried tomatoes, red peppers, artichokes and olives over a bed of greens. The Chicken Tortilla Salad (page 86) and Couscous Salad with Lemon-Soaked Grilled Chicken (page 84) are winners too, and work beautifully at get-togethers. You'll also find plenty of salads for weeknight meals, such as the BLT Chicken Salad or Crispy Chicken with Creamy Lemon-Parmesan Dressing. Please use these recipes as guidelines. Be inspired to borrow a different dressing or try new ingredients—and head off in your own direction.

Before you do, a small caveat. The most important element in a chicken salad is, of course, the chicken. It must be tender and juicy. Some specific cooking guidelines follow.

A few simple steps can guarantee perfectly cooked chicken every time.

When is the Chicken Done?

The perfect chicken salad has meat that is moist and tender. Whether roasted in the oven, poached in water or grilled, chicken should be removed from the heat when it's just done—that is, when the flesh turns from pink to white.

A meat thermometer can help take the guesswork out of tricky timing. It's okay to make a small cut in the chicken to test for doneness, but using an instant-read thermometer is even better. It will tell you precisely when a chicken is done (160° for breast meat).

After years of using cheap, but inaccurate and time-consuming dial thermometers, I purchased a Thermoworks Thermapen thermometer (the standard model: THS-211-006, $75). It was worth the investment since it's become one of my most useful kitchen tools for testing turkey, beef, pork and chicken.

Butterflying Chicken

A boneless chicken breast has both a thin and a thick end that can cause problems during cooking. By the time the thickest part is cooked, the thinner end is overdone. There are two ways to remedy this.

Pounding creates a cutlet of uniform thickness, so it cooks evenly. Use the flat side of a meat pounder or even a small cast iron or other heavy pan to do this. Pound the thicker end until it's closer in thickness to the thinner end.

An even easier method is to butterfly the chicken breast. Take a whole chicken breast and cut into two cutlets. Remove the tenderloin and trim the meat. Place each cutlet on a cutting board. With a knife held horizontally to the cutting board and one hand firmly placed on top of the chicken breast, carefully cut the thickest part of the breast almost in half making sure not to cut through the edge. Open up the meat like a book, creating a single flat piece. Use a meat pounder to completely flatten the chicken to uniform thickness.

Use the butterflied chicken for grilling or cooking in a skillet.

Quick Chicken Marinade

This is a simple marinade that takes little time to prepare. Place 1 pound of chicken breasts, or 2 cutlets, in a non-reactive bowl. Squeeze the juice of one lemon, about 2 to 3 tablespoons, over the chicken. Add 2 tablespoons olive oil, salt and pepper. It's nice to add 1 or 2 tablespoons of chopped fresh herbs, such as parsley, thyme, chives, tarragon or dill. Let the chicken marinate in the refrigerator, covered, for 30 minutes or longer—up to overnight.

Depending on the dish, you could also add mustard, garlic, shallots, soy sauce or another citrus such as orange or lime juice.

Roasting Split Chicken Breasts

Roasting split breasts (bone-in, with skin) provides moist, tender chicken for chicken salads in 35 to 40 minutes. I prefer this method over poaching. And while the chicken is roasting, you can prepare the salad.

The chicken can also be roasted a day ahead. One split breast yields about 1 cup cooked chicken that can be either shredded or diced, and you can cook as many as you need, which is easier and quicker than roasting a whole chicken each time you need the meat.

Preheat the oven to 350°. Place split breasts on a rimmed cookie sheet lined with tin foil for easy cleanup. Brush both sides with olive oil and sprinkle generously with salt. Roast for 35 to 40 minutes, or slightly longer for very large pieces, until chicken registers 160° on an instant-read thermometer. You can also check for doneness by making a small cut with a knife. When the meat turns from pink to white, the chicken is done.

Let chicken cool to room temperature, then remove the skin and bones. Now the chicken can be diced or shredded into bite-size strips along the grain.

Gas or Charcoal Grilling

Prepare the skinless, boneless chicken breast by removing the tenderloin and trimming the meat (save the tenderloin to grill with the breast). Pound the chicken with a meat pounder, or a small heavy skillet, to an even thickness. Or butterfly the chicken, following the instructions on page 72. This helps to keep the chicken moist because it cooks evenly.

If you are marinating the chicken first, add the ingredients, toss lightly to coat pieces, and marinate for 30 minutes or up to 24 hours prior to cooking. Marinating also helps to keep chicken moist.

Preheat an outdoor gas grill to medium-high, or start a charcoal grill. If you have not marinated the chicken, season it liberally with salt and pepper; brush with olive oil. Clean the grill grates when they're hot and lightly brush them with oil. Grill chicken 4 to 6 minutes on each side until grill marks appear and chicken is just cooked, 160° on an instant-read thermometer. When it's cool enough to handle, slice, shred or cube the chicken.

Stovetop Grilling

Stovetop grills or grill pans are excellent for quickly cooking chicken indoors. I find that the chicken doesn't dry out as easily as it sometimes does on an outdoor grill.

To use a stovetop grill pan, preheat it for several minutes over medium-high heat, until the grill is hot and chicken sizzles when placed on top. Brush the grill with oil. Season chicken with salt and pepper. Grill chicken 4 to 6 minutes on each side until grill marks form and chicken is just cooked, 160° on an instant-read thermometer. When it's cool enough to handle, thinly slice chicken on the diagonal.

Poaching

Poaching chicken in chicken broth results in a slightly tastier chicken. However, once dressed, it's hard to tell the difference between chicken that has been poached in stock or just water. It's up to you to decide.

Bring a quart of water or chicken stock to a boil in a large pan with a lid. If starting with a whole boneless, skinless chicken breast, cut it into two cutlets. Add the chicken to the water or stock, adding more liquid to cover the breasts if necessary. Turn the heat down so the water is just at a simmer. Aside from not overcooking, the key to perfectly poached chicken is cooking it at a gentle simmer. Boiling it will toughen the meat. Cover the pan and simmer the chicken, covered, for 5 or 6 minutes. Turn off heat and let the chicken rest in the pan for 6 to 8 minutes more, or until done. Cut into a piece to test for doneness or remove chicken from the pan when it registers 160° on an instant-read thermometer. Set chicken aside to cool. When it's cool enough to handle, dice or shred the chicken.

Poaching Bone-In Breasts

If you have a little extra time, or want to make the chicken ahead, this method provides moist, flavorful chicken, plus bonus chicken broth for another use.

Fill a large pot with about 3 quarts of water and add 5 or 6 split chicken breasts (bone in, with skin), 1 quartered onion, two celery stalks, 1 peeled garlic clove and either fresh parsley or fresh thyme sprigs, if you have them on hand. Bring water to a boil, lower the heat and simmer, partially covered, until chicken is cooked, about 15 to 20 minutes, or when it registers 160° on an instant-read thermometer. Be careful not to let the water boil, as it toughens the meat.

Remove chicken breasts from the pot (do not discard ingredients remaining in the pot). When it's cool enough to handle, remove meat from the bones and return the bones to the pot. Simmer this broth for an additional 30 minutes, then strain it well. When completely cool, refrigerate or freeze the broth. Makes 2 to 3 quarts.

Shred or dice the chicken depending on the recipe. Chicken can be stored in the refrigerator for up to 2 days, covered with plastic wrap.

Cooking Chicken Breasts in a Skillet

This is a quick way to cook a small amount of chicken to add to a salad, and if not overcooked, it can produce moist, tasty meat. Prepare chicken by removing the tenderloin. Place each cutlet on a cutting board. With a knife, carefully butterfly the chicken by following the instructions on page 72. Generously sprinkle both sides of the cutlets with salt and pepper.

Heat a heavy skillet or a cast-iron pan over medium-high heat until hot and add enough olive oil to coat the pan. Pan fry the cutlets, without moving them, until lightly browned on the first side, about 4 or 5 minutes. Turn and cook until the second side is lightly browned, another 3 or 4 minutes, or until just cooked through.

Remove chicken to a cutting board and let it rest for a few minutes (this will relax the fibers in the meat) before slicing or dicing it.

You can store cooked chicken in the refrigerator for up to 2 days.

CHICKEN SALAD WITH BOK CHOY, CELERY AND PEANUT-GINGER VINAIGRETTE

This is a delicious chicken salad with lots of vegetables, including mild-tasting, succulent bok choy and a light peanut sauce. It's best to add the dressing just before serving. Serve this on its own, or with the Thai Quinoa Salad on page 190.

3 split bone-in chicken breasts (with skin), or 3 cups cooked, shredded chicken

Olive oil

Salt

1/2 head bok choy (4 stalks), base trimmed off and stalks rinsed

1 carrot, peeled and cut into matchsticks

1 celery stalk, peeled, halved lengthwise and very thinly sliced

1 red bell pepper, cored and cut into very thin strips

2 tablespoons toasted sesame seeds

PEANUT-GINGER VINAIGRETTE

1/3 cup creamy-style peanut butter

3 tablespoons soy sauce

2 tablespoons honey

5 tablespoons fresh orange juice

2 tablespoons fresh lime juice

2 tablespoons canola oil

2 teaspoons minced fresh ginger

1/2 teaspoon minced garlic (optional)

1/4 teaspoon dried red pepper flakes or 1/8 teaspoon cayenne

1 Preheat the oven to 350°. Rub split chicken breasts with a little olive oil and season on both sides with salt. Place on a baking sheet and roast for 35 to 40 minutes, until just cooked. When chicken is cool enough to handle, remove the meat from the bone and shred by hand into thin strips. Refrigerate, covered, until ready to use.

2 Slice each bok choy stalk in half lengthwise. With your knife at a diagonal, cut each half into 1/4-inch slices, using both the white and green parts. Combine bok choy with the carrot, celery, and red pepper strips.

3 To make the dressing, in a medium bowl, whisk together all of the dressing ingredients.

4 Place the shredded chicken in a bowl and mix with the dressing. Then add the vegetables and mix lightly to coat. (Mixing the dressing with chicken first keeps the vegetables looking bright for a nicer presentation.) Top with toasted sesame seeds. The chicken and salad components can be prepared a day ahead and combined just before serving. Dress only the amount of salad you think you will serve that day.

VARIATION If you don't care for peanut dressings, try this salad with the Asian Vinaigrette on page 259.

CRISPY CHICKEN SALAD

This chicken—crispy on the outside and tender inside—is served with salad greens and Italian Lemon-Parmesan dressing. It's a family favorite, served at home or packed up for an outing. You can vary the salad by the season: field tomatoes and cucumbers in the summer or avocado, shredded red cabbage and red onion in the fall or winter.

CRISPY CHICKEN
4 boneless skinless chicken breast halves
Coarse salt and pepper
1/4 cup flour
1 egg
1 & 1/2 cups panko breadcrumbs
1/2 cup grated Parmigiano Reggiano cheese
2 tablespoons each butter and olive oil

SALAD
6 cups lettuce greens
1 carrot, peeled and sliced or julienned
1 cucumber, peeled and sliced
1 large tomato, cored and chopped, or about 1 cup cherry tomatoes, halved

LEMON-PARMESAN DRESSING
3 tablespoons fresh lemon juice
1/2 teaspoon minced garlic
2 tablespoons heavy cream, sour cream, crème fraîche or plain yogurt
2 tablespoons Parmigiano Reggiano cheese
1/2 teaspoon kosher salt
Pepper
6 tablespoons olive oil

1 Remove the tenderloin from each half of chicken breast and butterfly chicken, page 72. Cut each piece in half lengthwise, so you have 8 slender pieces of chicken, plus the tenderloin pieces. Season with salt and pepper on both sides.

2. Preheat the oven to 350°. Place flour on a plate, whisk egg in a medium bowl. On a separate plate mix breadcrumbs and Parmesan cheese. Dip each piece of chicken first in the flour, then in the egg, and then press firmly into breadcrumbs to evenly coat each side. Heat a large, heavy skillet over medium-high heat. Add 1 tablespoon each of butter and oil; when the oil sizzles place half of the chicken pieces in the skillet. Pan fry until golden, 2 or 3 minutes on each side. (The chicken may not be thoroughly cooked at this point.) Repeat the process with the other 4 pieces and the tenderloin, first removing any stray breadcrumbs in the pan with a paper towel. When all of the chicken is sautéed, place the cutlets on a baking sheet and bake until cooked through, about 6 to 8 minutes.

3 Combine the salad ingredients, except chicken; chill.

4 To make the dressing, in a small bowl, whisk the lemon juice, garlic, cream or yogurt, Parmesan cheese, and salt and pepper. Whisk in the olive oil until creamy.

5 Keep dressing separate until ready to serve. Place salad in a serving bowl or platter and add just enough dressing to coat. Top with chicken and drizzle with a bit more dressing. Or, you can pass the dressing separately.

SERVES 4

CHICKEN SALAD WITH FRUIT AND TOASTED PECANS

This is an easy chicken salad to make. Roasting the chicken breasts yields tender, moist chicken. For a luncheon or buffet, serve this salad in "cups" of Boston lettuce leaves, or on a platter surrounded with lettuce leaves. Pass a basket of rolls or bread separately.

3 split bone-in chicken breasts (with skin), or 3 cups cooked, diced chicken

Olive oil

Salt and pepper

1 crisp apple

1 firm but ripe pear

Lemon juice

1 cup seedless red grapes, halved

2 tablespoons chopped chives or parsley

1 cup toasted pecans, chopped

ORANGE-POPPY SEED DRESSING

1/3 cup mayonnaise

2 teaspoons apple cider vinegar

1 tablespoon honey

2 tablespoons fresh orange juice

1 tablespoon poppy seeds

1/2 teaspoon kosher salt

1 Preheat the oven to 350°. Rub split chicken breasts with a little olive oil and season on both sides with salt and pepper. Place on a baking sheet and roast for 35 to 40 minutes, until just cooked. When chicken is cool enough to handle, remove the meat from the bone and shred by hand or dice. Refrigerate, covered, until ready to use.

2 Core and dice the apple and pear. Sprinkle the fruit with 1 or 2 teaspoons of fresh lemon juice to keep it from discoloring. In a large bowl, combine the diced chicken, apple, pear, grapes and chives.

3 To make the dressing, in a small bowl, whisk together all of the dressing ingredients.

4 Just before serving, add all of the dressing to the chicken salad and toss well to combine. Adjust seasonings, adding additional salt if necessary. Top with the toasted pecans.

BLT CHICKEN SALAD WITH RANCH DRESSING

This chicken salad offers that great combination of bacon, lettuce and tomato. It's delicious with an herb ranch dressing, but you can substitute other dressings such as Blue Cheese or Basil-Balsamic on pages 252 and 242.

1 small head romaine or other lettuce (about 5 or 6 cups), washed and dried

1 cup frisée, washed, dried and torn into pieces (optional)

8 slices bacon

3 boneless, skinless chicken breast halves

1 avocado, sliced

2 tomatoes, diced, or 1 & 1/2 cups cherry tomatoes, quartered

2 cups garlic croutons (optional)

RANCH DRESSING

1/3 cup low-fat buttermilk

1/4 cup mayonnaise

2 tablespoons low-fat yogurt

1 clove garlic, finely minced

1 tablespoon apple cider vinegar

2 tablespoons canola oil

Salt and pepper

2 tablespoons minced fresh chives

1 Cut or tear the lettuce into bite-size pieces. Cook bacon until crisp; drain well on paper towels.

2 Heat a stovetop grill pan, skillet, or outdoor grill over medium-high heat. Pound the chicken breast halves to an even thickness, about 1/4- to 1/2-inch thick. Season with salt and pepper and brush with oil. Cook chicken about 4 or 5 minutes per side until just done. Let chicken rest on a cutting board for a few minutes before slicing into 1/2-inch wide strips.

3 Arrange the lettuce on a platter and combine with chicken strips. Top the salad with avocado slices, diced tomatoes and crumbled bacon. Add the croutons, if using.

4 To make the dressing, in a bowl, whisk together the buttermilk, mayonnaise, yogurt, garlic and vinegar. Whisk in oil until creamy. Season generously with salt, lots of pepper and chives. Serve the dressing on the side. If you're not serving the salad immediately, set the bacon and croutons aside separately; then add them and combine with the salad just before serving.

SERVES 6

CURRIED CHICKEN SALAD

Everyone loves my friend Rachel Vaughn's chicken salads. A private chef now living in Big Sky, Montana, her dressing of curry, mango chutney and fresh lemon juice combined with chicken, grapes and apples makes this salad addictive. Make sure your curry powder is fresh, not bitter-tasting.

4 split bone-in chicken breasts (with skin), or 4 cups cooked, shredded chicken

Juice of 1 lemon

Salt and pepper

3 to 4 celery stalks, finely diced

3 tablespoons chopped fresh chives

2 tablespoons chopped scallion

1/4 cup minced fresh parsley

2 cups seedless red grapes, halved or quartered

1 crisp apple, peeled and finely diced (sprinkled with lemon juice to prevent discoloration)

1/2 cup toasted pecans or sliced almonds

CURRY-MANGO CHUTNEY DRESSING

1 & 1/2 to 2 teaspoons curry powder

2 tablespoons mayonnaise

1/3 cup mango chutney, preferably Major Grey's

1/4 cup olive oil

Juice of 1/2 lemon

1/2 teaspoon pepper

1/2 teaspoon kosher salt

1 Preheat the oven to 350°. Rub split chicken breasts with lemon juice and salt and pepper. Place on a baking sheet, cover with foil, and bake for 35 to 40 minutes, until just cooked. When chicken is cool enough to handle, remove the meat from the bone and shred by hand into thin strips. Refrigerate, covered, until ready to use.

2 In a large serving bowl, combine the chicken, celery, chives, scallion, parsley, grapes and apple.

3 To make the dressing, in a small bowl, whisk together all of the dressing ingredients. Add dressing to the chicken salad and mix well to combine. Top with toasted nuts.

GRILLED CHICKEN SALAD WITH RED AND YELLOW PEPPERS AND HONEY-DIJON VINAIGRETTE

Tender, grilled chicken with crisp lettuce greens, colorful peppers and celery are dressed with a nicely balanced Honey-Dijon dressing. All ages, from kids to grandparents, like this one. I often serve it with a pasta salad, such as the one on page 153 and some grilled bread.

4 boneless skinless chicken breast halves

Juice of 1 lemon

2 tablespoons olive oil

1 tablespoon chopped fresh herbs, such as parsley, dill, tarragon, chives or thyme

1 head of lettuce, washed and dried

2 celery stalks, peeled, halved lengthwise and very thinly sliced

1 red bell pepper, cored and cut into thin strips

1 yellow bell pepper, cored and cut into thin strips

1/4 red onion, very thinly sliced

HONEY-DIJON VINAIGRETTE

2 tablespoons apple cider vinegar

2 tablespoons Dijon mustard

1 tablespoon plus 2 teaspoons honey

1 clove garlic, minced

1/2 cup olive oil

1/2 teaspoon kosher salt

Pepper

1 Remove the tenderloin from each cutlet and reserve. Pound the breasts to an even thickness, and marinate all the chicken in lemon juice, olive oil and herbs for at least 30 minutes or up to a few hours in the refrigerator. Meanwhile, tear the lettuce into bite-size pieces.

2 Preheat a stovetop grill pan or an outdoor grill. Remove chicken from the marinade and generously season with salt and pepper on both sides. Grill chicken 4 to 6 minutes on each side until grill marks form and chicken is just cooked, 160° on an instant-read thermometer. When cool enough to handle, thinly slice chicken.

3 To make the dressing, in a small bowl, whisk all of the dressing ingredients until creamy.

4 When ready to serve, place lettuce on a large serving platter and add just enough dressing to coat the leaves. Top with celery, peppers, red onion and the chicken slices. Drizzle additional dressing over the chicken and vegetables. Store any leftover dressing, covered, in the refrigerator.

SERVES 4 TO 6

COUSCOUS SALAD WITH LEMON-SOAKED GRILLED CHICKEN

This is a wonderfully light chicken and pasta salad from Christopher Osborn, former owner and chef of The Depot in Newton, Massachusetts. The rustic Italian couscous, cooked in broth instead of water, is rich with flavor. This dish can easily be made ahead and served cold, but its flavor is best when served at room temperature. For a vegetarian version, use vegetable stock in place of the chicken broth and serve with seasoned grilled vegetables such as portabella mushrooms, zucchini, summer squash and bell peppers sprinkled with fresh lemon juice.

CHICKEN

1 & 1/2 pounds of boneless skinless chicken breasts, sliced in half lengthwise

2 cloves garlic, crushed

1 teaspoon kosher salt

1 teaspoon pepper

2 tablespoons chopped parsley

Juice of 3 lemons, rinds reserved

COUSCOUS

1 pound Italian Couscous (Fregola Sarda)

5 cups chicken stock

1/2 cup minced Vidalia onion

8 ounces baby spinach, washed and dried

6 tablespoons olive oil

2 cloves garlic, crushed

2 tablespoons chopped parsley

Juice of 2 or 3 lemons

Pepper

1/2 cup grated Asiago or Parmigiano Reggiano cheese

Chopped scallions for garnish

1 lemon, thinly sliced

1 In a large bowl, toss chicken with garlic, salt, pepper and parsley, then squeeze the juice from the lemons over all. Add the reserved rinds, toss with the chicken mixture and let marinate for at least 2 hours in the refrigerator. Remove chicken from the marinade; discard marinade and lemon rinds.

2 Preheat an outdoor grill to high. Grill the chicken breasts over high heat, with the grill lid open, for about 7 to 9 minutes on one side. Do not move the chicken for at least 5 minutes—this allows the sugars to crystallize and form a nice brown crust. Turn the chicken and cook for an additional 5 minutes more, or until it is cooked through, 160° on an instant-read thermometer.

3 Cook the couscous in chicken stock according to package directions. When it is al dente, or just firm to the bite, remove couscous from heat and drain, leaving some of the starchy stock in the pot. Immediately add the onions and toss; then add the spinach and toss, and lastly, add the oil. Continue to toss pasta to help it cool faster and stop the cooking.

4 When couscous is cool, add the garlic, parsley, juice of 2 lemons and pepper. Test for flavor and add salt to taste; add additional lemon juice if needed. Transfer the salad to a serving platter and top with a sprinkling of grated cheese; garnish with scallions.

5 Serve atop or alongside the lemon-soaked grilled chicken and garnish with thinly sliced lemon.

ITALIAN COUSCOUS Italian couscous is a large toasted couscous about the size of tapioca pearls made from durum wheat semolina. It is available in some supermarkets or from specialty products importers as well as from some online sources. You can substitute Israeli or Middle Eastern couscous, the large but untoasted kind.

SERVES 4 TO 5

CHICKEN TORTILLA SALAD

The Mexican flavors of cilantro, lime and chiles add zest to this chicken salad, served with avocado, tomatoes and greens. It makes lunch for 3 or 4 pals or a fun, casual dinner. Arrange the colorful components in rows on a platter so that guests can serve themselves. Try a black bean or corn salad as an accompaniment.

3 split bone-in chicken breasts (with skin), or 3 cups cooked, shredded chicken

Salt and pepper

Juice of 1 lemon

6 corn tortillas (6 inches in diameter)

1 teaspoon olive oil

6 cups chopped romaine lettuce

2 cups shredded cheddar, Monterey jack, feta or goat cheese

2 avocados, sliced

2 tomatoes, diced or 1/2 pint cherry tomatoes, quartered

1/2 small red onion, slivered

LIME-CILANTRO DRESSING

1/4 cup fresh lime juice

1 jalapeño pepper, seeded

1 clove garlic

1/2 cup lightly packed cilantro leaves

1/2 cup olive oil

1/2 teaspoon kosher salt

Pepper

1 Preheat the oven to 350°. Rub split chicken breasts with salt and pepper and lemon juice. Place on a baking sheet and roast for 35 to 40 minutes, until just cooked. Leave oven on to toast the tortillas. When chicken is cool enough to handle, remove the meat from the bone and shred by hand into thin strips. Refrigerate, covered, until ready to use.

2 Cut tortillas in half, then cut each half into 1/4-inch strips. Place tortilla strips on a baking sheet, drizzle with a teaspoon of olive oil and sprinkle with salt. Bake until lightly crisp, turning occasionally with tongs, for about 10 to 12 minutes.

3 To make the dressing, combine all of the dressing ingredients in a blender and blend until smooth.

4 Place romaine on a large oval or rectangular serving platter. Arrange the remaining ingredients in rows on top of the greens on the platter: chicken, cheese, avocados, diced tomatoes, red onion and tortilla strips. Sprinkle the chicken and vegetables with salt and pepper. Serve the dressing on the side.

VARIATION Make wraps by using flour tortillas, skipping the corn tortilla strips in the original recipe. To spice up the dressing, add 1 canned chipotle pepper in adobo sauce and a touch of honey for balance.

SERVES 4

PESTO CHICKEN SALAD WITH BACON, TOMATOES AND GARLIC CROUTONS

Chicken coated with creamy pesto is topped with crunchy croutons and crispy crumbled bacon. I got the idea from the Vineyard Gourmet Shop on Martha's Vineyard, which makes a similar dish.

2 boneless, skinless chicken breast halves, or 2 cups cooked, shredded chicken
5 slices bacon
1/4 cup mayonnaise
1/4 cup pesto (prepared or homemade)
Salt and pepper
1 & 1/2 cups cherry tomatoes, quartered
1 & 1/2 cups garlic croutons, page 23

1 Bring 2 quarts of water to a boil in a medium saucepan. Cut each chicken breast into two cutlets. Add the chicken and turn down the heat so the water is just simmering. Do not allow the water to boil. Poach chicken, covered, for 5 or 6 minutes. Turn off the heat and let the chicken sit in the hot water for another 6 to 8 minutes, until just done. Remove chicken to a bowl, and when cool enough to handle, shred into small strips.

2 In a medium skillet set over medium-high heat, fry the bacon until crisp; drain on paper towels. When cool, crumble it into small pieces.

3 In a small bowl, mix the mayonnaise and pesto until well combined. Add to the chicken and mix well; season with salt and pepper to taste. Place the salad in a serving bowl. Season the tomatoes with salt and pepper and add them to the salad bowl along with croutons and crumbled bacon. If not serving immediately, set the croutons and bacon aside separately and add them just before serving.

"QUEEN OF HEARTS" RASPBERRY-CHICKEN SALAD

This recipe comes from Patti Powers and Ralph Legrande, owners of Cheshire Garden, which produces farmhouse mustards, fruit preserves and sauces, as well as a line of vinegars from fruit and herbs grown on their sustainable New Hampshire farm. Their "Queen of Hearts" Raspberry Vinegar is a 50/50 blend of dark red raspberries and vinegar with a touch of honey—and since I first tried it 10 years ago, I've been hooked. Use a fine-quality store-bought raspberry vinegar if you can't locate "Queen of Hearts."

3 boneless skinless chicken breast halves

1/4 cup, plus 2 tablespoons "Queen of Hearts" or other raspberry vinegar

Salt and pepper

1/4 cup minced red onion

1/4 cup finely diced red bell pepper

1/4 to 1/3 cup mayonnaise

4 cups mixed salad greens, washed and dried

1 to 3 tablespoons olive oil

1 cup fresh raspberries

1 kiwi, peeled, sliced and quartered

1 Place chicken breasts in a heavy skillet, pour 1/4 cup of vinegar over them and simmer, covered, over medium-low heat, for 5 to 7 minutes on each side until done, or until an instant-read thermometer registers 160°. When cool enough to handle, cut the meat into cubes or shred it, and season with salt and pepper. Refrigerate uncovered until completely cool.

2 Place chopped onion and bell pepper in a bowl with 1/4 cup mayonnaise and 1 tablespoon raspberry vinegar. When chicken is cool, add it to the bowl and mix well. Taste for seasoning and add more salt or mayonnaise if necessary.

3 When ready to serve, arrange the mixed greens in a bowl or on a platter. In a small bowl, mix the remaining tablespoon of vinegar with 1 to 3 tablespoons oil and a pinch of salt. (You'll probably need more oil with store-bought vinegar.) Dress the salad greens and top them with the chicken salad. Top with fresh raspberries and kiwi.

VARIATIONS Experiment with different garnishes—instead of raspberries or kiwi, you might try orange sections, avocado slices, fresh chopped chives, or chopped, toasted nuts such as pecans or hazelnuts.

PROVENÇAL CHICKEN SALAD WITH ROASTED PEPPERS AND ARTICHOKES

With bits of sun-dried tomatoes, roasted peppers, artichokes and olives, this chicken salad makes a great presentation and tastes fantastic. A little shaved Parmesan or fresh mozzarella could be added, if desired. Serve with some crusty or peasant-style bread.

1/2 cup sun-dried tomatoes
1 can (14 ounces) artichoke hearts
4 boneless, skinless chicken breast halves
Salt and pepper
1 roasted red bell pepper, cut into strips
1/2 cup pitted French green olives, sliced lengthwise into quarters
3 tablespoons minced parsley
4 cups mixed baby lettuce greens, washed and dried

DIJON-HERB VINAIGRETTE
2 tablespoons red wine vinegar
2 teaspoons Dijon mustard
1/2 teaspoon minced garlic
6 tablespoons olive oil
1 teaspoon dried oregano
1/2 teaspoon kosher salt
Pepper

1 Place sun-dried tomatoes in a small bowl and cover with boiling water. Let rest until softened, about 10 to 15 minutes. Drain tomatoes and mince them. Rinse the artichoke hearts and cut into quarters, then pat dry with paper towels.

2 Preheat a stovetop grill pan, outdoor grill or skillet over medium-high heat. Remove tenderloins from the chicken breasts and pound the chicken to an even thickness. Season with salt and pepper. Oil the grill and either grill or pan fry the chicken 4 or 5 minutes on each side until just cooked. When cool enough to handle, slice into 1/2-inch wide strips.

3 In a large bowl, combine the chicken, sun-dried tomatoes, roasted pepper, artichoke hearts, olives and parsley.

4 To make the dressing, in a small bowl, whisk all of the dressing ingredients; season with pepper. Before serving, whisk dressing again and combine with the chicken salad.

5 To serve, place baby greens on a platter and top with the chicken salad or serve on individual plates. The vinaigrette from the salad will seep through to flavor the greens below.

VARIATIONS To serve this as a vegetarian meal, omit the chicken and substitute just grilled or roasted vegetables such as zucchini, yellow squash and eggplant. Use fresh tomatoes in place of sun-dried tomatoes if they're in season. Try different herbs such as chives, basil and dill along with, or instead of, parsley.

SERVES 4 TO 6

ROASTED CHINESE CHICKEN WITH SNOW PEAS AND WATER CHESTNUTS

It's the contrast of moist tender chicken with the crunchy snap of snow peas and water chestnuts that makes this salad so satisfying and visually pleasing. The recipe is from friend and chef Rachel Vaughn, who tops the salad with a spicy Chili-Citrus dressing. It's easy enough to make anytime, and impressive enough to serve on special occasions.

3 split bone-in chicken breasts (with skin), or 3 cups cooked, shredded chicken
Salt and pepper
Juice of 1 lemon
3 cups snow peas, strings removed
1 can (8 ounces) sliced water chestnuts, rinsed well and drained
1 red bell pepper, cored and cut into thin strips
3 tablespoons chopped fresh chives
3 cups baby greens
Pita bread

CHILI-CITRUS DRESSING
1 teaspoon rice vinegar
3 tablespoons fresh lemon juice
Grated zest of 1 orange
1 tablespoon fresh orange juice
Grated zest of 1 lime
1 tablespoon fresh lime juice
2 tablespoons hot chili oil (not hot sesame oil)
2 tablespoons honey
1/2 teaspoon red pepper flakes
1/2 teaspoon kosher salt
1/2 cup canola or grapeseed oil
Pepper

1 Preheat the oven to 350°. Rub split chicken breasts with salt and pepper and lemon juice. Place on a baking sheet, cover with foil, and roast for 35 to 40 minutes, until just cooked. When chicken is cool enough to handle, remove the meat from the bone and shred by hand into thin strips. Refrigerate, covered, until ready to use.

2 Blanch the snow peas in boiling water for 30 seconds; drain and place in a bowl filled with cold water and ice to stop the cooking, or run under cold water. Dry well on paper towels.

3 Combine the snow peas, water chestnuts, red pepper, chives and chicken in a bowl.

4 To make the dressing, in a small bowl, whisk together all of the dressing ingredients, seasoning to taste with pepper. Refrigerate the dressing and salad separately until ready to serve.

5 To serve, mix dressing with chicken salad. Place baby greens on a platter and top with chicken salad. Cut pita bread into quarters and place around the edges of the platter.

TARRAGON CHICKEN SALAD WITH GRAPES

Roasted chicken with red grapes and fresh tarragon make a quick but delicious salad in this recipe from Karen Dutton, manager of Tea Lane Caterers on Martha's Vineyard.

2 whole boneless skinless chicken breasts
Salt and pepper
2 tablespoons chopped fresh tarragon
3/4 to 1 cup mayonnaise
1 & 1/2 cups seedless red grapes, halved
**1 or 2 heads butterhead or leafy lettuce
(optional)**
6 mini rolls (optional)

1 Preheat the oven to 400°. Cut each chicken breast into 2 halves and season generously with salt and pepper. Place on a baking sheet and roast for about 20 minutes, until just cooked. When cool enough to handle, pull chicken into shreds.

2 Mix the shredded chicken with the tarragon, mayonnaise and grapes; season well with salt and pepper to taste. Serve in lettuce "cups" or on mini rolls.

MAIN COURSE MEAT SALADS

MAIN COURSE MEAT SALADS

The all-in-one meal is the hallmark of this chapter, in which salad greens, vegetables and beef or lamb are united by their own special vinaigrettes or dressings. The recipes range from casual meals to composed platters that can feed a crowd. I love the simplicity and great flavor of the Tomato and Arugula Salad with Grilled Steak and Portabella Mushrooms. This salad works especially well in summer when tomatoes are in season and people are inclined to fire up their outdoor grills. The Grilled Flank Steak with Chimichurri Sauce, a spicy, fresh herb dressing with South American flair, makes a gorgeous presentation for company. The platter is filled with strips of juicy grilled steak, roasted corn, black beans, leafy greens, and red onions, and all of these elements are enhanced by the chimichurri sauce. There's something about grilled foods meeting up with a flavorful dressing that brings out the best of both.

If you like Greek Salads, try the Grilled Lamb Skewers and Romaine Salad. The accompanying sauce made with yogurt, cucumbers, lemon and garlic is one of my favorite condiments.

The kinds of greens and vegetables used in these salads can vary widely, from a mix of green lettuces to a combination of lettuce with colorful radicchio, feathery frisée or endive. The Mixed Greens and Radicchio Salad with a Gremolata Dressing features greens, cucumbers and sweet grilled red onions. You can vary the recipe by adding grilled eggplant, zucchini, or roasted artichokes too. So borrow the ideas and the dressings I've shared with you in this chapter and think about which other ingredients will also partner well in your own creations.

GRILLED FLANK STEAK WITH ROASTED CORN, TOMATOES AND CHIMICHURRI SAUCE

The national steak sauce of Argentina, chimichurri combines lots of fresh herbs—especially parsley—with garlic, oil and vinegar or citrus. Here, it dresses thinly sliced grilled steak that's served over a salad along with oven-roasted corn, tomatoes, black beans and greens. Chimichurri is a good sauce for fish, too!

Kernels from 3 ears of corn
1 flank steak, about 1 & 1/4 to 1 & 1/2 pounds
Salt and pepper
Olive oil
1 red onion, cut into wedges
5 cups lettuce greens of your choice, washed and dried
2 cups cherry tomatoes, quartered, or 2 tomatoes, cut into wedges
1 can (14 ounces) black beans, rinsed
1 lime, quartered, for garnish

CHIMICHURRI SAUCE
3 tablespoons red wine vinegar
3 tablespoons chopped shallots
2 teaspoons minced garlic
3/4 cup lightly packed fresh parsley leaves
1/4 cup fresh basil leaves
2/3 cup olive oil
1/2 teaspoon red pepper flakes
Salt and pepper

1 To make the sauce, combine all of the ingredients for the Chimichurri Sauce in a blender. Pulse 3 or 4 times to combine, but leave the mixture slightly chunky. Taste and adjust the salt and pepper, if necessary.

2 Preheat the oven to 350°. Line a rimmed cookie sheet with parchment paper and spread the corn kernels on it in a single layer. Spoon 1 or 2 tablespoons of the Chimichurri Sauce over the corn, mix, and roast until cooked, about 8 to 10 minutes.

3 Preheat a stovetop grill pan or outdoor grill. Season the steak with salt and pepper on both sides and brush with oil. Grill until meat is medium-rare, about 5 to 7 minutes on each side, depending on the size of the steak. Brush onion wedges with olive oil and grill alongside the meat. When the steak is done, place it on a cutting board and brush with 1 or 2 tablespoons of the Chimichurri Sauce, then let it rest for at least 5 minutes before very thinly slicing it diagonally, against the grain.

4 Place greens on a large serving platter. Arrange the tomatoes, black beans and corn on different areas of the platter, leaving room in the center for the meat. Place the sliced steak and onions on the salad in the center of the plate. Garnish with lime wedges. Pass the Chimichurri Sauce separately to spoon over individual portions.

SPICY THAI STEAK AND NAPA CABBAGE SALAD

Napa cabbage adds a light crunchiness to this dish. Lots of mint and cilantro along with a vibrant, oil-free lime dressing add the Thai-flavor notes. If you have basil on hand, toss it in, too. The thinner you slice the cabbage and vegetables, the more appealing they are.

2 tenderloin or rib-eye steaks (about 1 & 1/2 pounds), or any cut you prefer
Salt and pepper
4 cups very thinly sliced Napa cabbage (1 small to medium head)
1 carrot, peeled and julienned or shredded
1 cucumber, peeled, seeded and sliced
1 red bell pepper, cored and thinly sliced
1/2 small red onion, thinly sliced
1/2 cup fresh cilantro, chopped
1/3 cup fresh mint, chopped

THAI DRESSING
1/2 cup lime juice
2 tablespoons sugar
2 tablespoons Asian fish sauce
1/4 to 1/2 teaspoon red pepper flakes

1 Season the steak with salt and pepper on both sides. Heat a grill or heavy pan.

2 In a medium bowl, combine the shredded cabbage, carrot, cucumber, red pepper and red onion. Toss in the herbs and mix well.

3 In a small bowl, combine all of the dressing ingredients and mix well to dissolve the sugar. Set aside.

4 Grill or pan-fry the steaks to the desired degree of doneness. Let the steaks rest on a cutting board for at least 5 minutes while you dress the salad. Save some of the dressing to drizzle on steak, along with any juices that have accumulated on the cutting board. Slice the steaks. Divide the salad among 2 to 4 plates, place the slices on top of each serving and drizzle the remaining dressing over all.

SERVES 2

TOMATO AND ARUGULA SALAD WITH GRILLED STEAK AND PORTABELLA MUSHROOMS

This salad makes an easy weeknight dinner, but is special enough for casual entertaining. Add some roasted rosemary potatoes and grilled garlic bread to complete the meal. Arugula tastes great here, but any local mix of salad greens works equally well. For cheese lovers, top with a little crumbled gorgonzola or blue cheese.

1/2 teaspoon minced garlic
2 tablespoons olive oil
2 portabella mushrooms, brushed clean, stems removed
1 New York strip or rib-eye steak (about 14 to 16 ounces)
Salt and pepper
4 cups arugula, washed and dried
1 or 2 tomatoes, cut into small wedges

BALSAMIC VINAIGRETTE
1/2 teaspoon minced garlic
2 tablespoons balsamic vinegar
1 teaspoon fresh lemon juice
5 tablespoons olive oil
Salt and pepper

1 In a small bowl, mix 1/2 teaspoon of garlic and 2 tablespoons oil. Brush some of the mixture on the mushrooms first, and then on the steak. Sprinkle mushrooms and steak liberally with salt and pepper; set aside. Start the grill, either gas, charcoal or stovetop grill pan, over medium-high heat.

2 In another small bowl, make the vinaigrette by mixing 1/2 teaspoon garlic with the vinegar and lemon juice. Whisk in 5 tablespoons oil. Add salt and pepper to taste.

3 Grill the steak and mushrooms to desired doneness. Let the steak rest on a cutting board while you prepare the rest of the salad. Place arugula on a serving platter and top with tomatoes. Thinly slice the grilled mushrooms and scatter them throughout the salad. Slice steak across the grain into strips and add to salad. Drizzle the steak, tomatoes and mushrooms with the vinaigrette and sprinkle with a little additional salt and pepper.

SERVES 4

MINI BEEF BURGERS AND LEAFY GREEN SALAD WITH BLUE CHEESE DRESSING

My boys—my husband and my son—love beef, so I like to find ways to combine vegetables and leafy greens with steak and hamburgers. This dish fits the bill, and is easy to make on a weeknight. I use whatever in-season vegetables I have on hand for the salad: big beefy tomatoes and cucumbers in the summer; red cabbage, celery and red onion in the fall.

BURGERS

1 pound ground chuck (85 percent lean)
2 tablespoons chopped scallion
1 tablespoon Worcestershire sauce
2 teaspoons Dijon mustard
1/3 cup breadcrumbs, preferably panko
1/2 teaspoon kosher salt
1/2 teaspoon pepper

SALAD

1 small head lettuce or 4 cups mixed greens
1 ripe tomato, cored and cut into chunks
1 cucumber, peeled, halved lengthwise and sliced
1/2 red onion, very thinly sliced
1/4 cup blue cheese, crumbled

BLUE CHEESE DRESSING

1/4 cup blue cheese
2 tablespoons heavy cream, milk or crème fraîche
2 tablespoons lemon juice
5 tablespoons olive oil
1/4 teaspoon kosher salt
Pepper

1 In a medium bowl, combine the beef, scallions, Worcestershire sauce, mustard, breadcrumbs and salt and pepper. Form into 8 burger patties. Refrigerate.

2 In a large bowl, combine the salad greens, tomato, cucumber and red onion. To make the dressing, in a food processor or blender, combine the blue cheese, heavy cream or milk, lemon juice and oil. Process until dressing is creamy; season with salt and pepper.

3 Grill or pan-fry the hamburgers to the desired degree of doneness. Place the burgers on individual plates and add a portion of salad alongside each. Drizzle each salad portion with the dressing. Crumble blue cheese over burgers and salad.

MIXED GREENS AND RADICCHIO SALAD WITH GRILLED SLICED STEAK

The mixture of parsley, garlic and grated lemon zest is known as gremolata. Here, it's been transformed into a vinaigrette that contributes concentrated flavor to leafy greens topped with grilled steak and red onions.

5 cups mixed baby greens or arugula, washed and dried
1 cup thinly sliced radicchio (optional)
1/2 medium cucumber, peeled, cut in half lengthwise, and thinly sliced
1 & 1/2 to 2 pounds steak for grilling, such as strip, sirloin or tenderloin
Salt and pepper
1 red onion, cut into 6 wedges
Olive oil

GREMOLATA DRESSING
2 teaspoons grated lemon zest
1 teaspoon finely minced garlic
2 tablespoons finely minced fresh parsley
2 tablespoons fresh lemon juice
5 tablespoons olive oil
Salt and pepper

1 Place the baby greens or arugula and radicchio, if using, on a serving platter or in a large bowl. Top with cucumber slices and refrigerate until ready to serve.

2 Preheat a stovetop grill pan or outdoor grill. Season steak with salt and pepper on both sides, season onion wedges with salt, and brush both well with olive oil. When grill racks are hot, brush them with olive oil and grill the onions, turning to cook evenly, alongside the steak. Let the steak rest for 5 to 10 minutes on a cutting board.

3 To make the dressing, in a small bowl, combine the lemon zest, garlic, parsley and lemon juice. Whisk in the oil and generously season with salt and pepper.

4 Place grilled red onion wedges on top of the salad. Thinly slice the steak and add to salad. Pass the dressing separately.

VARIATIONS You can substitute other vegetables or toppings for the salad in place of cucumbers, especially grilled tomatoes, artichokes, eggplant, summer squash, zucchini or even potatoes.

GRILLED LAMB SKEWERS WITH HERBED YOGURT SAUCE

This is an all-in-one meal with luscious grilled lamb, romaine salad, pita bread and a creamy herbed yogurt sauce.

1 & 1/2 pounds boneless leg of lamb, cut into 1-inch chunks

Salt and pepper

Olive oil

1 small head romaine lettuce (about 4 or 5 cups), washed, dried, torn or chopped into bite-size pieces

1/4 red onion, thinly sliced

1/2 medium cucumber, peeled and sliced

1/2 cup pitted Greek olives, sliced

1 cup cherry tomatoes, quartered, or 1 tomato, chopped

Pita bread

GREEK VINAIGRETTE

1 tablespoon fresh lemon juice

1 tablespoon red wine vinegar

1 teaspoon dried oregano

5 tablespoons olive oil

Salt and pepper

HERBED YOGURT SAUCE

1 & 1/2 cups plain whole milk yogurt, drained through a paper coffee filter for 20 minutes

1/2 medium cucumber, peeled, seeded, then cut into 1/4-inch dice

1 tablespoon olive oil

2 teaspoons fresh lemon juice

1/2 teaspoon finely minced garlic

1/2 teaspoon ground cumin

1/4 cup chopped fresh cilantro or mint

Salt and pepper

1 Thread the lamb chunks onto 6 skewers, (if using wood skewers, soak them in water for 30 minutes before using), season with salt and pepper and brush well with oil. In a medium bowl, combine the romaine, red onion, cucumber, olives and tomatoes; chill until ready to serve. To make the dressing, in a small bowl, whisk together the lemon juice, vinegar, oregano, oil, and salt and pepper.

2 When the yogurt is drained, place it in a bowl and stir in the diced cucumber, oil, lemon juice, garlic, cumin and cilantro. Add a pinch of salt and pepper.

3 Preheat a stovetop grill pan or outdoor grill and cook the lamb skewers for 3 or 4 minutes on each side for medium-rare. Cut into one of the pieces: the center should be pink. While lamb is grilling, wrap the pita bread in foil and warm them in the oven. When lamb is done, dress the romaine salad with the vinaigrette and cut the pita bread into quarters. Place the salad on a serving platter and arrange the lamb skewers on one side; pita bread on the other. Pass the yogurt sauce for the lamb separately.

SEAFOOD SALADS

SEAFOOD SALADS

Salads with seafood are among my favorite dishes. Crisp vegetables and tender pieces of fish make a satisfying combination, especially when enhanced with a flavorful homemade vinaigrette. A vinaigrette is like adding lemon to fish; the bright flavors and slight acidity just make the fish taste better. The vinaigrettes in this chapter serve as flavorful sauces for the fish and as dressings for the accompanying salad.

Some of the seafood salads veer from the traditional leafy greens. The Cajun Shrimp and Corn Salad combines seasonal corn and diced fresh tomatoes with seared hot shrimp flavored with garlic and a Cajun spice mix. I've brought this salad to several potlucks, and people love it! The Tuna "Niçoise," Asian-Style, is a little different also, combining seared tuna with daikon and edamame. Served with the accompanying citrus vinaigrette, the dish is fresh and light. It makes a good dinner or lunch entrée. For other casual entertaining ideas, try the avocados stuffed with shrimp, or lobster salad served atop crispy fried tomatoes.

Somewhere along the way, I discovered that salsas, which make ideal toppings for fish, can be transformed easily into vinaigrettes, creating even more options. All it takes is adding oil and vinegar or citrus in roughly the same proportions as with any other dressing. For example, a spicy-sweet mango salsa vinaigrette can be spooned atop seared salmon and tender mixed greens. The bits of red onion, tomato, jalapeño pepper, fresh lime juice and cilantro in the salsa vinaigrette add plenty of flavor and complexity to the dish. Similarly, a tomato and olive mixture becomes a full-flavored vinaigrette with the addition of red wine vinegar, olive oil, garlic and herbs. Both dressings are at home with all kinds of seafood, including halibut, swordfish, shrimp and scallops.

You can experiment a bit with these salads. If you don't have a particular ingredient or fish that's on the list—aside from maybe the vinegar and oil—substitute something else. You can get creative, or simply pare down to the essentials. Your choices will help to invent unique new salads.

Most of these recipes can be made year-round, but many lend themselves to casual summertime dining, out on the porch or in the backyard near the grill.

SERVES 4 TO 6

CAJUN SHRIMP AND CORN SALAD WITH LIME-CHILE DRESSING

In the summer, some of my friends organize a potluck dinner every Saturday night at Squibnocket Beach. They're the kind that always include lots of kids, sizzling grilled food, great salads and a fire to toast marshmallows for s'mores. Before one August night's potluck, I mixed corn and tomatoes from Morning Glory Farm with some Cajun-spiced shrimp and a simple lime juice and olive oil dressing. It was gone before you could say Squibnocket three times.

1 & 1/4 pounds medium shrimp, peeled and deveined

2 to 3 teaspoons Cajun seasoning

2 tablespoons olive oil

1 teaspoon minced garlic

1/4 teaspoon red pepper flakes or 1/8 teaspoon cayenne

Kernels from 6 ears of corn (about 3 cups)

1/2 pint cherry tomatoes, halved

1 roasted red bell pepper, cored and diced (optional)

2 tablespoons minced fresh parsley

LIME-CHILE DRESSING

2 tablespoons fresh lime juice

1 teaspoon ancho chile powder

1 tablespoon olive oil

Salt and pepper

1 In a medium bowl, combine the shrimp and Cajun seasoning. Heat oil in a very large skillet (or use two large skillets) over medium-high heat. Add the shrimp, cook for a few minutes, then add the garlic and red pepper flakes or cayenne and finish cooking; a total of about 4 to 6 minutes. Meanwhile, steam the corn kernels for 3 or 4 minutes. Let the shrimp and corn cool to room temperature.

2 In a large serving bowl, combine the shrimp, corn, tomatoes, roasted red pepper and parsley. In a small bowl, combine all of the dressing ingredients and add to the salad. Mix well and taste for any seasoning adjustments such as more lime juice, salt or pepper. Serve the salad at room temperature.

VARIATION To make this salad go even further, add cooked large Israeli couscous or orzo. You will need to increase or even double the amount of lime juice and olive oil.

SERVES 2 TO 3

SEARED TUNA WITH WHITE BEAN, FENNEL AND ARUGULA SALAD

A vinaigrette featuring tomatoes and olives is spooned over just-cooked fresh tuna on a bed of arugula, white beans, and slivers of fennel. Coating the fresh tuna in a prepared spice mix, such as Cajun, lemon pepper or jerk, gives it a tasty crust when cooked.

1 small fennel bulb with top
4 cups baby arugula, washed and dried
1 cup cooked white beans
1 pound fresh tuna steak, cut into 2 portions
Salt and pepper
2 tablespoons dry spice mix of your choice
1 tablespoon canola oil

TOMATO-OLIVE VINAIGRETTE
2 tablespoons red wine vinegar
2 tablespoons fresh lemon juice
1/2 teaspoon minced garlic
2/3 cup olive oil
1/2 cup seeded and finely diced tomatoes
3 tablespoons chopped pitted kalamata olives
1 tablespoon minced fresh parsley or basil
Salt and pepper

1 Slice off the fennel bulb top; chop and reserve 1 to 2 tablespoons of the feathery fronds. Cut the fennel bulb into quarters and remove the core. Using a very sharp knife or a mandoline, slice the fennel into slivers. You will need about 1 cup. Place arugula on individual plates and top with the fennel slices, white beans and chopped fennel fronds. Cover and refrigerate until ready to serve.

2 To make the dressing, in a medium bowl, combine the vinegar, lemon juice and garlic. Slowly whisk in the olive oil. Add the chopped tomatoes, olives, parsley or basil, salt and pepper to the vinaigrette.

3 Season the tuna on both sides with salt and pepper. Place dry spice mix on a plate and dredge tuna on both sides, coating evenly. Heat a heavy sauté pan, such as cast iron, over medium-high heat. Add the oil and sear tuna on one side for about 3 or 4 minutes or until a nice 1/4-inch thick crust forms. Turn the tuna, and sear on the other side, another 2 to 4 minutes. Thinly slice tuna across the grain and arrange over the arugula and fennel. Generously spoon the dressing over the tuna and salad.

AVOCADOS STUFFED WITH SHRIMP SALAD

You can stuff avocados with tuna, crab or shrimp salad for an easy—and tasty—presentation. I recommend buying one additional avocado in case another is bruised when opened.

1 tablespoon Old Bay seasoning

1 pound medium shrimp, peeled and deveined

3/4 cup cucumber, peeled, seeded and cut into 1/4-inch dice

2 tablespoons chopped fresh dill

1 tablespoon chopped fresh chives

2 avocados

Salt

4 cups mixed baby salad greens, washed and dried

LEMONY DRESSING

Grated zest of 1 lemon

3 tablespoons fresh lemon juice

3 tablespoons olive oil

3 tablespoons mayonnaise

Salt and pepper

1 In a large saucepan, bring 4 or 5 cups of water and the Old Bay seasoning to a boil. Add the shrimp, lower heat, and simmer, covered, for 1 minute. Turn off the heat and let shrimp rest, covered, in the hot water for 3 minutes more, or until they are pink and opaque. Drain, and let cool in the refrigerator.

2 When shrimp are cool, cut them into 1/2-inch chunks. Place them in a bowl with the diced cucumber, dill and chives.

3 To make the dressing, in a small bowl, whisk together the lemon zest, lemon juice and oil. Whisk in mayonnaise until the dressing is creamy. Generously season with salt and pepper. Reserve 1 tablespoon of dressing for the greens and combine the rest with the shrimp salad. Refrigerate until ready to serve.

4 To assemble the salad, cut the avocados in half and remove the pits. Scoop out a bit of the avocado to make the cavity slightly larger. Season with salt. Top each avocado half with a mound of shrimp salad. (You may have some shrimp salad left over.) Toss salad greens with the reserved dressing and arrange on a platter or on individual plates. Nestle the avocado halves in the salad.

SERVES 2

115
·
RAISING
THE
SALAD
BAR
·

SEARED SCALLOPS WITH WATERCRESS AND WARM ORANGE DRESSING

Friend and chef Rachel Vaughn and I created this dish during scallop season on Martha's Vineyard. The scallops are complemented with bright bursts of pineapple, crunchy radishes and a blood orange vinaigrette.

1 large bunch watercress (2 to 3 cups), or other salad greens, washed and dried

2 tablespoons olive oil

Salt and pepper

1 teaspoon light vinegar (Champagne, rice, Moscatel)

1/2 cup diced fresh pineapple

2 radishes, trimmed and very thinly sliced

3/4 pound sea scallops, membranes removed, rinsed and patted dry

2 lemon wedges

WARM ORANGE DRESSING

Juice of one blood orange or tangerine, about 1/2 cup

1 tablespoon light vinegar (Champagne, rice, Moscatel)

1 teaspoon maple syrup or pinch of sugar

1 Remove the thicker stems from the watercress and roughly chop the rest of the bunch. In a bowl, toss the watercress with 1 tablespoon of the oil and a pinch or two of salt. Sprinkle with 1 teaspoon of vinegar. Place salad greens on a serving platter or on 2 individual plates and top with the pineapple and radishes.

2 Heat a large, heavy skillet over medium-high heat; when hot, add the remaining tablespoon of oil. Sear the scallops for 2 or 3 minutes on each side, taking care to brown each side but not overcook. Sprinkle salt on each side of the scallops during cooking. Remove scallops from pan and arrange on the salad. To make the dressing, add the orange or tangerine juice, remaining tablespoon of vinegar and maple syrup to the same pan, set on high, and bring to a boil. Cook until liquid is slightly reduced and thickened, about 3 or 4 minutes.

3 Grind some fresh pepper and squeeze a little lemon juice over the salad. Drizzle the sauce over and around the scallops. Serve immediately while scallops are still hot.

SERVES 4

SEARED SALMON AND NAPA CABBAGE WITH WARM LEMON-SOY DRESSING

In this recipe, the salmon goes right from the oven to a bed of fresh shredded Napa cabbage and vegetables; then it's bathed in a warm dressing of ginger, lemon and soy. The recipe also works with baby spinach, watercress, mixed greens or arugula, if Napa cabbage is unavailable.

4 cups very thinly sliced Napa cabbage (about 1/4 head) or baby spinach

4 scallions, thinly sliced

1/2 thick carrot, peeled and cut into matchsticks

2 radishes, trimmed and cut into matchsticks or 1/2 cucumber, peeled, seeded, and thinly sliced

4 salmon fillets (about 6 ounces each, with skin)

Salt and pepper

1 tablespoon canola or vegetable oil

1 In a serving bowl, combine the cabbage, scallions, carrot, and radishes or cucumber.

2 Preheat the oven to 375°. Heat a heavy ovenproof skillet, preferably cast iron, over medium-high heat. Season the salmon with salt and pepper. Add 1 tablespoon oil to the pan, then add the fish fillets, flesh side down. Cook undisturbed until salmon is lightly browned, about 3 to 5 minutes. Carefully slide a spatula under each fillet and turn over. Transfer the skillet to the oven to finish cooking, approximately 6 to 8 minutes, or until the fish is almost opaque throughout, but still moist.

3 While fish is cooking, make the dressing. In a small skillet, heat 3 tablespoons oil and add the ginger. Let ginger sizzle for about 1 minute. Stir in the soy sauce and lemon juice, then turn off the heat.

4 Divide the salad among 4 individual plates and drizzle each serving with a little dressing. Remove fish from the skillet, discarding the skin that remains in the pan. Arrange a salmon fillet in the center of each salad and spoon the remaining dressing over all.

VARIATION   I sometimes include delicate-tasting arame seaweed to this salad. I love the look of the thin black strands with the pale Napa cabbage and pink salmon. Arame is a little hard to measure in its dried form, but soak about 1/4 to 1/3 cup of it in boiling water. Drain and add to the salad. You'll usually find arame in the Asian section of the supermarket, alongside other types of seaweed like nori. Sprinkle on some toasted sesame seeds as a finishing touch.

LEMON-SOY DRESSING

3 tablespoons canola or vegetable oil

1 & 1/2 teaspoons finely minced fresh ginger

2 tablespoons soy sauce

2 tablespoons fresh lemon juice

SERVES 4

SEARED SALMON WITH BABY GREENS AND MANGO SALSA VINAIGRETTE

By transforming a mango salsa into a sweet, spicy vinaigrette, you have both a sauce for the fish and a dressing for the leafy greens. It will complement any chicken or fish dish that favors mangoes and tomatoes, such as shrimp, halibut and swordfish.

4 salmon fillets (about 6 ounces each), with skin
Salt and pepper
1 tablespoon canola oil
6 cups mixed baby greens, washed and dried

MANGO SALSA VINAIGRETTE
2 tablespoons red wine vinegar
2 tablespoons fresh lime juice
1 & 1/2 teaspoons honey
6 tablespoons olive oil
2 tablespoons minced red onion
1 tablespoon minced, seeded jalapeño pepper
1/2 teaspoon finely minced garlic
1/2 teaspoon ground cumin
1 ripe mango, cut into 1/4-inch dice (about 1 cup)
1/2 cup finely diced, seeded tomato
1/4 teaspoon kosher salt
2 or 3 tablespoons chopped cilantro leaves

1 To make the vinaigrette, in a medium bowl, combine the vinegar, lime juice and honey. Add the oil in a slow, steady stream, whisking constantly until dressing is emulsified. Add the red onion, jalapeño pepper, garlic, cumin, mango, tomato and salt; combine. Stir in cilantro leaves. If not using the dressing immediately, cover it and store in the refrigerator. Bring the dressing to room temperature before serving.

2 Preheat the oven to 350°. Season salmon with salt and pepper. Heat the oil in an oven-proof skillet, preferably cast iron, over medium-high heat. Add the salmon, flesh side down, and sear until a golden brown crust forms, about 3 to 5 minutes. Carefully slide a spatula under each fillet and turn over. Transfer the skillet to the oven to finish cooking, approximately 6 to 8 minutes, or until salmon is almost opaque throughout, but still moist. Try not to overcook.

3 Divide baby greens among 4 individual plates. Carefully lift the salmon fillets, leaving the skin in the skillet, and place one fillet at the center of each plate. Whisk the vinaigrette and generously spoon it over the fish and greens.

EASY TOMATO SEEDING Cut off the top of a regular-sized tomato or cherry tomato, turn upside down over sink and gently squeeze out seeds. For larger tomatoes, cut in half and gently squeeze seeds from either half. For this recipe, after seeding, cut into strips and cut strips into a tiny dice.

SERVES 4 TO 6

GRILLED SHRIMP SALAD WITH WATERMELON, HERBS AND FETA CHEESE

Make this cooling salad in high summer when both fresh, ripe tomatoes and watermelon are at their peak.

1 & 1/2 pounds medium or large shrimp, peeled and deveined, tails left on

3 medium tomatoes, halved, seeded and cut into 1-inch chunks

2 medium cucumbers, peeled, seeded, and cut into 1/2-inch chunks

3 cups 1-inch watermelon chunks, seeds removed

1/2 cup pitted kalamata olives, quartered lengthwise

1 tablespoon chopped fresh dill

1 tablespoon finely chopped fresh mint

1 tablespoon minced fresh parsley

1/2 pound feta cheese, cut into 1/2-inch cubes

1 cup baby arugula or micro-greens

VINAIGRETTE

3 tablespoon fresh lemon juice

1 tablespoons red wine vinegar

1/2 teaspoon finely minced garlic

6 tablespoons olive oil

Salt and pepper

1 To make the dressing, in a small bowl, combine the lemon juice, vinegar, garlic, and olive oil. Season with salt and pepper.

2 Place the shrimp in a medium bowl. Mix the dressing again and add 2 tablespoons of the dressing to the shrimp. Marinate in the refrigerator for 10 minutes.

3 In a large bowl, combine the tomatoes, cucumber, watermelon, olives, and herbs; set aside.

4 Preheat a grill or stovetop grill pan. (If using an outdoor grill, you might want to skewer the shrimp for easier handling. If you use wood skewers, be sure to soak them in water for 30 minutes before using.) Grill the shrimp, 2 to 3 minutes on each side, or until they turn from translucent to pink.

5 Just before adding the remaining dressing to the salad, drain excess liquid from the tomato-watermelon mixture. Whisk the dressing again and add it to the salad. Gently mix in the feta cheese and arugula or micro-greens. Transfer the salad to a serving platter and top with shrimp.

SERVES 4

121
·
RAISING
THE
SALAD
BAR
·

PAN-ROASTED HALIBUT WITH TOMATO-OLIVE VINAIGRETTE

Try this luscious olive and tomato vinaigrette with other fish as well—swordfish, salmon, striped bass and shrimp love it, too.

4 halibut fillets (6 to 8 ounces each) with skin

Salt and pepper

1 tablespoon olive oil

6 cups mixed baby greens, washed and dried

1 lemon, cut into wedges

TOMATO-OLIVE VINAIGRETTE

2 tablespoons red wine vinegar

2 tablespoons fresh lemon juice

1/2 teaspoon finely minced garlic

2/3 cup olive oil

1/2 cup seeded and finely chopped tomatoes

3 tablespoons chopped pitted kalamata olives

1 tablespoon minced fresh parsley

Salt and pepper

1 Preheat the oven to 350°. Generously season each piece of halibut with salt and pepper. Heat an oven-proof sauté pan, preferably cast iron, over medium-high heat. Add the oil; then place the fish, flesh side down, in the pan and cook for 4 or 5 minutes, until golden brown. Carefully turn over the fish fillets and transfer the pan to the oven. Bake until fish is done, approximately 10 minutes for a 1-inch thick fillet.

2 To make the dressing, in a medium bowl, mix the vinegar, lemon juice and garlic. Slowly whisk in olive oil until dressing is emulsified. Stir in the chopped tomatoes, olives, parsley, and salt and pepper.

3 Place the greens in a large bowl and toss with a spoonful or two of the dressing. Divide the salad among 4 individual plates. Place a piece of fish on top of each serving and generously spoon the remaining dressing over each piece. Serve with a wedge of lemon.

STEAMED MUSSELS WITH GARLIC CROUTONS AND MICRO-GREENS

Pour Lemon-Garlic dressing over hot mussels, top with crispy croutons and spicy micro-greens, and you have a delicious appetizer or first course. If micro-greens are unavailable, chop another spicy green like arugula or watercress into small pieces, or used chopped parsley.

2 pounds fresh mussels, scrubbed and rinsed well

1 & 1/2 cups micro-arugula or other spicy micro-green

2 cups homemade garlic croutons, page 23

LEMON-GARLIC DRESSING

3 tablespoons olive oil

2 cloves garlic, finely minced

3 tablespoons fresh lemon juice

Salt and pepper

1 To make the dressing, heat a small skillet over low to medium heat. Add the oil and garlic and sauté until garlic is fragrant, 1 or 2 minutes. Remove from heat and add the lemon juice, parsley, salt and pepper.

2 Cook the mussels just minutes before you are ready to serve them: In a large pot, bring an inch of water to a boil. Add the mussels, reduce heat slightly, and cook the mussels, covered, until they open, about 4 to 6 minutes, depending on their size. Drain well, using the cover of the pot to hold the mussels in. Discard any mussels that haven't opened. Place the greens in a small bowl, and have ready nearby.

3 Whisk the dressing and drizzle a little of it over the greens; gently toss. Pour the rest of the dressing over the mussels in the pot and mix to coat. Gently mix in the greens and garnish with croutons. You can either serve the mussels in one large bowl or in individual bowls. If serving individually, make sure you include some liquid from the bottom of the pot.

SERVES 4

SEARED TUNA SALADE NIÇOISE

Without the potatoes and anchovies, this Niçoise salad veers from the traditional version but still provides an appealing make-ahead meal. Adorned with slices of fresh-seared tuna, baby greens, tomatoes, thin green beans, artichokes and olives, it's a taste and texture sensation. Dredging the fresh tuna in a prepared spice mix, such as Cajun, lemon pepper, or jerk, gives it a tasty crust when cooked. Try this with poached shrimp in place of tuna, too. If you do, omit the seasoning mix.

1 to 1 & 1/2 pounds fresh tuna steak, cut into 2 or 3 pieces
Salt and pepper
2 tablespoons dry spice mix of your choice
1 tablespoon canola oil
1 can (14 ounces) artichokes, rinsed, drained and quartered
1 small clove garlic, minced
1 tablespoon olive oil
1/4 pound French green beans (haricots verts), ends trimmed
4 to 5 cups mixed baby greens, washed and dried
1/2 cup pitted Niçoise or other black olives
1 & 1/2 cups cherry tomatoes, quartered or halved
1/4 red onion, thinly sliced

DIJON-HERB DRESSING
2 tablespoons red wine vinegar
2 teaspoons fresh lemon juice
1 teaspoon Dijon mustard
1/2 teaspoon each dried oregano, basil and thyme
1/2 teaspoon minced garlic
1/2 cup olive oil
Salt and pepper

1 Season the tuna steaks with salt and pepper. Place dry spice mix on a plate and dredge the tuna on both sides. Heat a heavy sauté pan, preferably cast iron, over medium-high heat. Add the oil and when it's hot, sear tuna on one side for about 3 to 4 minutes or until a nice 1/4-inch thick crust forms. Turn the tuna steaks, and sear them on the other side, another 2 to 4 minutes. Let cool slightly, then refrigerate, uncovered, until ready to serve.

2 Preheat the oven to 400°. Take the artichokes, pat dry with paper towels and place them on a baking sheet lined with parchment paper. Toss the artichokes with minced garlic and 1 tablespoon oil and roast until their edges begin to crisp, about 15 to 20 minutes.

3 Steam the green beans for 4 or 5 minutes, then run under cold water to stop the cooking.

4 To make the dressing, in a medium bowl, whisk the vinegar, lemon juice, mustard, herbs and garlic. Slowly add the olive oil, whisking constantly. Generously season with salt and pepper.

5 Arrange the salad greens on a large serving platter. Add the olives, tomatoes, artichokes, red onion and green beans, giving each their own section of the platter, leaving room for the tuna. Carefully cut the tuna steaks against the grain into thin slices and arrange them on the platter. Pass the dressing separately.

SERVES 4

125
·
RAISING
THE
SALAD
BAR
·

TUNA "NIÇOISE," ASIAN-STYLE

Asian-style salade Niçoise: fresh-seared tuna with leafy greens, edamame, crisp daikon radish slices and delicate arame seaweed. Though some of these ingredients may be unfamiliar, they're easy to put together and can be re-worked to serve 2 on a weeknight. In that case, halve the ingredients, but use the same dressing.

1 to 1 & 1/2 pounds fresh tuna steak, cut into 2 or 3 pieces
Salt and pepper
2 tablespoons dry spice mix of your choice
1 tablespoon canola oil
1/2 cup dried arame seaweed
1 cup fresh or frozen edamame beans
1 section daikon radish (about 3 inches) or 6 red radishes
Sections from 2 or 3 navel oranges
1/2 cucumber, peeled, seeded and thinly sliced
4 or 5 cups mixed baby salad greens, or a mix of arugula, frisée, watercress or mâche
2 tablespoons toasted sesame seeds

ASIAN CITRUS DRESSING

3 tablespoons canola or peanut oil
1 tablespoon rice vinegar
2 tablespoons fresh lime juice or lemon juice
3 tablespoons orange juice
1 tablespoon honey
1 teaspoon finely-minced fresh ginger
1 tablespoon soy sauce

1 Season tuna with salt and pepper on both sides. Place spice mix on a plate and dredge the tuna on both sides, pressing lightly so the spice mix adheres. Heat a heavy sauté pan, preferably cast iron, over medium-high heat. Add the oil and when it's hot, sear the tuna on one side for about 3 or 4 minutes, or until a 1/4-inch thick crust forms. Turn and sear on the other side, another 2 to 4 minutes. Let cool slightly, then refrigerate, uncovered, until ready to serve.

2 Bring a medium saucepan of water to a boil. Place arame in a small bowl and add some of the boiling water. Add edamame beans to saucepan and cook for 3 or 4 minutes. Run edamame under cold water to stop cooking; drain well. Soak arame for 15 minutes; drain well.

3 Peel the daikon radish. Slice, on a diagonal, into very thin ovals. Slice each oval into thin matchsticks.

4 In a jar with a lid, combine all of the dressing ingredients and shake vigorously to dissolve the honey.

5 Arrange the salad greens on a large serving platter. Add edamame, orange sections, daikon radish, arame and cucumbers giving each on their own section of the platter, leaving room for the tuna. Carefully cut the tuna against the grain into thin slices and arrange on the platter. Pass the sesame seeds and dressing on the side. Each person should re-shake the dressing before pouring.

VARIATIONS Try toasted nori seaweed, cut into thin strips, instead of the arame. You can also add sliced avocado, bean sprouts, sliced scallion greens and sliced red onions.

SERVES 4

GOLDEN FRIED TOMATO WITH LOBSTER SALAD AND AVOCADO PUREE

This popular lobster salad was developed by chef Keith Korn and sous chef Job Yacubian during the summer of 2001 at the former Ice House Restaurant on Martha's Vineyard. The same place is now known as Bittersweet, with Job as the chef/owner. He still keeps the popular dish on the menu, not only on its own merits, but also as an homage to his good friend and cooking mentor.

LOBSTER SALAD
2 cups cooked, shelled lobster meat, diced
3 tablespoons celery and celery leaves, finely diced
2 to 3 heaping tablespoons Hellmann's mayonnaise
1 teaspoon each of fresh chives and tarragon
Dash of ketchup
Salt and pepper

FRIED TOMATO
1 large ripe tomato, preferably yellow or another low-acidity variety
Flour
1 egg, beaten
Panko breadcrumbs
Vegetable or corn oil

AVOCADO PUREE
1 large, very ripe avocado, pitted and peeled
Dash of olive oil
1 teaspoon chopped fresh cilantro
Salt and pepper

Lemon zest, celery leaves, sliced radishes, chopped chives, or basil oil for garnish (optional)

1 In a medium bowl, combine all of the lobster salad ingredients; chill.

2 Slice tomato into 4 slices each about 1/2-inch thick. Dust each slice in flour on both sides and shake off excess, then dip into beaten egg and coat in the panko breadcrumbs. Heat up to 1/2 inch of oil in a skillet and pan-fry the tomato slices until golden brown on both sides. Drain on paper towels.

3 In a food processor, puree the avocado, oil, cilantro, and salt and pepper until mixture is very smooth. Add a tiny bit of water if necessary. Cover and chill.

4 When ready to serve, place a heaping tablespoon of avocado puree on 4 individual plates. Top puree with a slice of fried tomato, then spoon a generous portion of lobster salad on top. (Use a 1/2-cup dry measure to mold and shape the lobster salad, if desired.) Garnish each serving with lemon zest, tender celery leaves, thinly sliced radish or chives. Drizzle a little basil oil around the plate, if desired.

SERVES 4

SWORDFISH KABABS WITH LEMON-PARSLEY VINAIGRETTE

These swordfish kababs get a simple, delicious coating of parsley and spices. Mince all of the parsley and garlic at the same time for both the fish rub and the dressing.

SWORDFISH KABABS
1 & 1/2 pounds swordfish, 1-inch thick
1/3 cup minced parsley
1 teaspoon minced garlic
1 teaspoon ground cumin
2 teaspoons paprika
Salt and pepper
Wood skewers, soaked in water for 30 minutes
2 tablespoons olive oil

SALAD
6 cups mixed baby salad greens, washed and dried
1 & 1/2 cups fresh pineapple, cut into bite-size pieces

LEMON-PARSLEY VINAIGRETTE
2 tablespoons fresh lemon juice
5 tablespoons olive oil
2 teaspoons grated lemon zest
1/2 teaspoon finely minced garlic
2 tablespoons chopped parsley
Salt and pepper

1 Cut the swordfish into 1-inch chunks. In a medium bowl, mix the parsley, garlic, cumin and paprika. Add the swordfish chunks and toss well to thoroughly coat them. Generously season with salt and pepper. Thread the fish onto skewers. Preheat the grill.

2 To make the vinaigrette, in a small bowl, whisk together the lemon juice and oil, then add the lemon zest, garlic, parsley, and salt and pepper.

3 When the grill racks are hot, oil them well and grill the swordfish skewers on all 4 sides, about 10 to 12 minutes, turning often. Place the salad greens on a large serving platter. Top with fresh pineapple and swordfish skewers. Pass the dressing separately to use on both the swordfish and the salad.

RADICCHIO AND ENDIVE SALAD WITH SMOKED BLUEFISH

This is a beautiful first-course salad with a mix of magenta, dark green and pale green lettuces. The centerpiece is smoked bluefish—either slices of it or smoked bluefish pâté spread on sliced baguette. Smoked bluefish is abundant where I live, but if it is unavailable you can easily substitute smoked trout or smoked salmon.

1/2 small head radicchio, cut into quarters and cored

1 endive, cut in half lengthwise and cored

1 bunch watercress or baby arugula (about 2 cups), washed and dried

1/2 cucumber, peeled, cut in half lengthwise and seeded

1 pound smoked bluefish, or 1 half-pint container smoked bluefish pâté

1 baguette (if using the pâté)

1 lemon or lime, cut into wedges

LEMON-LIME DRESSING
6 tablespoons olive oil
1 & 1/2 tablespoons capers, rinsed
1 tablespoon fresh lemon juice
1 tablespoon fresh lime juice
1/2 teaspoon minced garlic
Salt and pepper

1 Slice the radicchio quarters into thin strips. There should be about 1 cup. Slice the endive lengthwise into thin strips. (Soak radicchio and endive in cold water for 10 minutes to remove some of the bitterness, if desired.)

2 Remove any large stems from the watercress leaving their smaller stems intact. Delicately chop the watercress by making a few random slices through the entire bunch. Cut each cucumber half crosswise into thin slices. Combine the radicchio, endive, watercress or arugula and cucumber in a bowl. Cover, and refrigerate until ready to serve.

3 To make the dressing, in a small skillet set over medium heat, combine 1 tablespoon of the oil and the capers, letting the capers sizzle for 2 or 3 minutes. In a small bowl, whisk together the lemon juice and lime juice, garlic and remaining 5 tablespoons oil. Season with salt and pepper, then and add the capers, including the oil they were cooked in.

4 Just before serving, quickly whisk the dressing and add just enough to coat the salad. Mix well.

5 Divide the salad among 4 individual plates. Place a section of smoked fish on top of each serving and drizzle a little more dressing over them. Include a wedge of lemon or lime with each serving. If using pâté, slice a fresh baguette and spread each slice with pâté. Arrange two or three pieces on each plate.

NOT YOUR MOTHER'S POTATO SALADS

Summer is when we most enjoy a good potato salad. It's also harvesting time: potatoes are at their peak of taste and flavor, a good time to seek out smaller, newer ones.

With the many varieties of potatoes in supermarkets and especially at farmers markets or local farmstands, you can make just as many different potato salads. When I worked for Martha's Vineyard chef Tina Miller, she would make a beautiful salad mixture of new red, purple and yellow potatoes that she picked up weekly at the farmers market. Dressed with a mustard vinaigrette, this salad tasted as fabulous as it looked. (Her recipe is on page 143.)

The farmers market is where I first discovered fingerling potatoes, the narrow, oblong potatoes with a buttery flavor. There are different varieties of fingerlings, some waxier, firmer and tastier than others—three qualities that are ideal for a potato salad. They cook quickly and don't easily fall apart. Fingerlings can now be found in supermarkets, though they are generally pricier than the typically used red potato.

Once the kind of potato has been chosen, the next major decision is the choice of dressing and other ingredients. Fresh herbs, nuts, sun-dried tomatoes, green beans, asparagus and leafy greens lend color and zest to potato salads. In my previous book, *Greens, Glorious Greens*, we paired potatoes with arugula, tomatoes and a mustard and white wine vinegar dressing. In this chapter, Boston chef Burke Forster takes that salad a step further, adding goat cheese and crisp bacon to his version. Just as warm potato dishes love cream or sour cream, potato salads have an affinity for creamy ranch-style and blue cheese dressings and, of course, mayonnaise.

Potato salads can also include sweet potatoes. The best sweet potato salad I've ever had was at Café DiCocoa in Bethel, Maine. Owner Cathi DiCocco generously shared her recipe, which pairs roasted sweet potatoes with corn and black beans and a chipotle pepper-sweet chile dressing.

Experiment a little in the summer and explore a whole new world of potato salads. Start right here.

BEST POTATOES FOR SALADS

134
·
RAISING
THE
SALAD
BAR
·

Red Potatoes

Red potatoes are most commonly used in potato salads. They are low in starch, considered to be the waxiest, and are easy to slice. Red potatoes also have a delicate flavor and thin skins. Select small red potatoes that are uniform in size, and cook them whole with their skins on. If different varieties of small red potatoes are available, try Red Gold, Rose Gold, Desiree or Cranberry Red.

Fingerling

Fingerling potatoes have a distinctive shape: small, narrow and oblong. They can be yellow-skinned or rosy-skinned with the firm, waxy consistency that you want for making potato salads. Cook them whole, in their skins. Different fingerling varieties have different qualities—some have a buttery flavor, but others can be drier and blander, so it's a good idea to experiment with a few fingerlings in your market to find a favorite. These varieties make good potato salads: Russian Banana, LaRatte or La Reine, Austrian Crescent, Ozette and French Fingerling.

Golden Potatoes

Yellow-fleshed potatoes can vary in flavor; some are waxier and contain more starch than others. Because of these characteristics, some varieties will work well in a potato salad while others will not. Some, though, can have superior flavor, so it's worth sampling a few of the smaller varieties to find one that's suitable. Try Bintje, Carola, Concord and some Yukon Golds.

Blue or Purple Potatoes

Blue- or purple-skinned potatoes can be combined with other potato varieties in a salad as a striking accent, especially the ones that are purple throughout, (that is, flesh and skin). These are namely the All-Blue or Purple Peruvian.

Use Potatoes that are Uniform in Size

To ensure even cooking, purchase potatoes that are roughly the same size so they'll all reach doneness at the same time. Small red potatoes that measure about 1 to 1 & 1/2 inches are a good size.

POTATO SALAD 101

135
·
RAISING
THE
SALAD
BAR
·

For potato salads, boiling and steaming are the cooking methods of choice. Both methods take about the same amount of time. To keep potatoes from falling apart or becoming water-logged, cook the potatoes, especially the smaller ones, whole, in their skins.

Boiling

Fill a large pot with cold water. Add scrubbed whole potatoes and bring water to a boil. Reduce heat to medium-high and gently boil the potatoes until they're tender, usually about 15 to 20 minutes for potatoes less than 2 inches in diameter. Test one of the potatoes for doneness by piercing it with the tip of a paring knife; it should slide in easily. Cool potatoes slightly under running water to allow easy handling.

Steaming

Steaming works best for medium-starch potatoes such as Yukon golds or all-purpose white potatoes. Use a saucepan with a steamer insert and fill the saucepan with water up to the bottom of the insert. Scrub the potatoes while you bring the water to a boil. Add potatoes to the steamer insert and cook, covered, until tender, about 15 to 20 minutes. If you have more potatoes than will fit in the steamer in a single layer, cook them in batches. Cool potatoes slightly under running water to allow easy handling.

Use Fresh Herbs

Chopped fresh herbs surround each potato with flavor. Try parsley, dill, chives, chervil, basil, tarragon and oregano, alone or in combination with each other.

Some Good Dressings

These particular dressings take a special fancy to potato salads: Basic-Balsamic, Tomato-Olive Vinaigrette, Blue Cheese, Honey-Mustard, Green Goddess, Fresh Herb Vinaigrette, and Creamy Lemon-Walnut (without the Parmesan). See the Vinaigrettes chapter starting on page 233 for these recipes.

Cutting the Potatoes

As you cut potatoes, bits of cooked potato build up on your knife and make it harder to get a nice clean cut without breaking the potato. After every few slices, wipe the knife blade with a damp paper towel.

Serve Potato Salads at Room Temperature

Potato salads that use vinaigrettes, as opposed to mayonnaise-based dressings, taste best at room temperature, dressed just before being served. If you want to prep ahead of time, make the dressing, chop any vegetables and scrub the potatoes. Store each component separately, and simply cook the potatoes on the same day you are serving them.

SERVES 6 TO 8

MEXICAN SWEET POTATO AND BLACK BEAN SALAD

One of our frequent outdoor vacation destinations is Bethel, Maine, home of Sunday River Ski Resort and one of our favorite eating spots: Café DiCocoa. The café's ever-changing breakfast and lunch menu can include fresh peach scones, homemade bagels, vegetable frittatas, soups and a variety of salads, all made with fresh ingredients by a very creative chef/owner, Cathi DiCocco. One café favorite is this combo of roasted sweet potatoes, corn and black beans with a unique chipotle-sweet chile dressing.

4 medium sweet potatoes, peeled and cut into 3/4-inch chunks

2 tablespoons canola oil

1/2 teaspoon ground coriander

1/2 teaspoon ground cumin

1/2 teaspoon chile powder

1/2 teaspoon kosher salt

Kernels from 3 to 4 ears of fresh corn, or 2 cups frozen kernels

2 cups cooked black beans, rinsed and drained (canned is fine)

3 or 4 scallions, thinly sliced

1/2 cup chopped cilantro

CHIPOTLE-CHILE DRESSING

1 chipotle chile (from a can of chipotles in adobo)

1 clove garlic, finely minced

2 tablespoons Thai sweet chile sauce (such as Maesri brand)

6 tablespoons fresh lime juice

1/2 cup canola oil

1 Preheat the oven to 375°. In a large bowl, toss the sweet potato chunks with the oil to lightly coat them. Sprinkle with coriander, cumin, chile powder and salt and toss again. Spread the potatoes in a single layer on a rimmed baking sheet and roast until they are golden at the edges and just tender, about 20 to 25 minutes. Meanwhile, microwave the corn in a small amount of water for 3 to 5 minutes, or steam for 3 or 4 minutes. Drain excess water. In a large serving bowl, combine the corn and black beans.

2 To make the dressing, in a blender or food processor, place the chipotle chile, garlic and sweet chile sauce. Process until mixture is smooth. Add the lime juice and process again. With the machine running, slowly add the canola oil and process dressing until it is emulsified.

3 When the sweet potatoes are done, let cool slightly and add them to the corn and beans. Add scallions and cilantro; gently toss. Pour enough dressing over the salad to just moisten the ingredients and toss again.

VARIATIONS See next page for more of Cathi's tips.

CATHI DICOCCO'S VARIATIONS FOR MEXICAN SWEET POTATO AND BLACK BEAN SALAD

This hearty dish can be:

• Served chilled and mounded on a bed of fresh greens

• Rolled into a soft flour tortilla with fresh spinach to make it a wrap

• Layered onto a flour tortilla with shredded cheese, then folded and grilled until golden to make it a quesadilla

• Incorporated into your favorite chili recipe, with added tomatoes and onions

Cathi's Kitchen Notes:

• The dressing can be made in large quantities and frozen in small containers for future use

• Blend the dressing with canned beans to make a smoky bean dip

• Use dried black beans if you want to cook up an extra batch for another use. Freeze family-size portions in doubled zipper-type plastic bags

• Substitute canned diced tomatoes for the sweet potatoes, and it's a wicked good salsa!

POTATO AND GREEN BEAN SALAD WITH DILL PESTO

This potato-green bean combo tastes best on the day it's made, dressed just before serving. You can make another version of this salad by using basil pesto instead.

1 & 1/2 pounds small red-skinned or fingerling potatoes

1/2 pound French green beans (haricots verts), trimmed and cut in half or thirds

DILL PESTO

1 clove garlic

1/4 cup lightly-packed fresh dill

2 tablespoons chopped fresh parsley

1 & 1/2 tablespoons apple cider vinegar

2 teaspoons Dijon mustard

1/3 cup olive oil

Salt and pepper

1 Fill a large saucepan with cold water and potatoes and bring to a boil. Lower heat to medium and cook until they can be easily pierced with a knife, about 15 minutes. Drain and let cool. Cut the potatoes into quarters.

2 Steam the green beans for about 4 minutes, then drain and run them under cold running water until they're cool to the touch. Combine with potatoes in a serving bowl.

3 To make the pesto, in a food processor, add the garlic clove and mince. Stop the machine and then add the other pesto ingredients. Process until mixture is well combined. Just before serving, add enough pesto to coat the potatoes and green beans. This potato salad tastes best served at room temperature.

SERVES 6 TO 8

POTATO SALAD WITH ARUGULA, TOMATOES, BACON AND GOAT CHEESE

Boston chef Burke Forster hits a home run with this colorful, delicious potato salad. It's a perfect accompaniment for a brunch or a backyard barbecue. This salad tastes best on the day it's made, and dressed just before serving so the arugula won't wilt.

2 pounds small (about 1 to 1 & 1/2 inches) red potatoes

Salt

4 slices thick-cut bacon, cut into 1-inch pieces

1 cup cherry tomatoes, halved

1/3 cup pitted kalamata olives, halved (optional)

1 & 1/2 cups baby arugula, washed and dried, coarsely chopped

4 ounces goat cheese

BALSAMIC DRESSING

2 tablespoons balsamic vinegar

4 tablespoons olive oil

Salt and pepper

1 Boil potatoes in a large pot of salted water until they are tender and can be easily pieced with a knife, about 13 to 15 minutes. Cool potatoes slightly under running water to allow easy handling. While still warm, cut the potatoes into quarters and place them in a large serving bowl; season with salt. Cook the bacon and drain well on paper towels.

2 To make the dressing, in a small bowl, whisk together the vinegar and oil, and generously season with salt and pepper. When potatoes have cooled to room temperature, add the tomatoes, olives, if using, and arugula. Place goat cheese in the freezer for five minutes, then crumble it with a fork.

3 When ready to serve, pour the dressing over the salad and gently combine. Taste and adjust seasonings if necessary. Garnish with bacon and goat cheese.

FINGERLING POTATO SALAD WITH BALSAMIC-MUSTARD VINAIGRETTE

Oblong and narrow, fingerling potatoes make great potato salads because of their taste and easy slicing. They can be cut in half on the diagonal or into smaller pieces. Baby spinach can stand in for the frisée if it's not available.

1 & 1/2 pounds fingerling potatoes, scrubbed
Salt
2 cups frisée, washed, dried and torn into pieces
1/4 small red onion, thinly sliced
1/2 cup toasted walnuts, chopped

BALSAMIC-MUSTARD VINAIGRETTE
1 & 1/2 tablespoons balsamic vinegar
2 teaspoons Dijon mustard
1/2 teaspoon maple syrup
1/4 cup olive oil
Salt and pepper

1 Fill a large pot with cold water, add the potatoes and bring to a boil. Reduce heat to a low boil and cook potatoes until they can be easily pierced with a knife, about 12 to 15 minutes. Slightly cool potatoes under running water to allow easy handling. Cut the potatoes on a diagonal into 1/2- to 3/4-inch pieces and place in a serving bowl. Season with salt.

2 In a small bowl, combine all of the dressing ingredients, whisking until thoroughly blended. Pour the dressing over the potatoes and mix well. Add the frisée, red onion and walnuts and gently mix. Serve at room temperature.

SERVES 6

143
·
RAISING
THE
SALAD
BAR
·

HERBED NEW POTATO SALAD

New potatoes are just young potatoes—they're harvested early and are small in size. They are very sweet and tender, and do not need peeling, which makes them perfect for potato salad. Martha's Vineyard chef Tina Miller looks for different color varieties such as Peruvian, fingerling and cranberry for a stunning multi-colored dish. This salad is made with a Dijon vinaigrette, and is best when it's served warm or at room temperature. Tina is the author of *Vineyard Harvest: A Year of Good Food on Martha's Vineyard*, one of my favorite cookbooks.

2 pounds new potatoes, such as fingerling, red, and/or purple

DIJON VINAIGRETTE
2 tablespoons apple cider vinegar
1/4 cup olive oil
2 tablespoons Dijon mustard
Salt and pepper
2 tablespoons chopped fresh chives
2 tablespoons chopped fresh parsley
2 tablespoons chopped fresh dill

1 To make the vinaigrette, in a small bowl, whisk the vinegar, oil, mustard, and salt and pepper to taste, then add the chopped herbs.

2 Fill a large pot with cold water, add the potatoes and bring to a boil. Reduce heat to medium and cook, uncovered, for 10 to 15 minutes, depending on the size of the potatoes, until they are tender and can be easily pierced with a knife. Remove pot from heat; drain. Set potatoes aside and let them cool just enough to handle, about 5 minutes. Slice the warm potatoes in half and place them in a serving bowl. Gently toss with the vinaigrette before serving.

PERFECT PASTA SALADS

PERFECT PASTA SALADS

I think of pasta salads as crowd pleasers—especially when the crowd is hungry! Open a box of pasta and cook it in just minutes, add vegetables and you're on your way. Adding fresh vegetables to pasta salads is an enjoyable way to bolster your diet, and they also help your salad become more than just pasta.

The most important issue in creating pasta salads is flavoring the pasta, which, on its own, is a rather bland canvas. Many cooks make the mistake of not adding enough other ingredients, especially vegetables or herbs. Another common error is to add raw vegetables—broccoli, zucchini, mushrooms and green beans—which could all benefit from some quick cooking to bring out their flavors.

Checking for vegetables in season is a good starting point because they provide the most flavor. In spring, consider combinations of the first green vegetables such as asparagus, artichokes, fava beans, peas and watercress. A spring pasta dish in this chapter marries asparagus and artichoke hearts with bow-tie pasta, shreds of lemon zest and tangy sheep's milk feta cheese.

In summer, perfectly ripe tomatoes, fresh corn kernels, fragrant torn basil and fresh mozzarella mingled with pasta is one of my most popular combinations. When these ingredients are around, especially tomatoes for the juiciness, sweetness and mild acidity they bring to pasta, there are so many salad possibilities. Greek-style pasta salad can be cooling on a hot summer night, with a little saltiness from the olives and cheese to balance the sweetness of the summer vegetables. (I like this salad to beat out winter blues too, if I can find some flavorful cherry tomatoes.) Fresh herbs are everywhere in the summer and you can easily toss in combinations of chopped fresh parsley, dill, oregano, basil, summer savory, mint or even a tiny bit of rosemary. Speckled throughout a pasta salad, herbs lend flavor and color.

Finally, don't overlook the many mild-tasting Asian vegetables that are ideal for pasta salads: Napa cabbage, bok choy, snow or snap peas, and a new favorite: edamame or fresh soy beans. The udon salad partners edamame with shrimp, and gets a real kick from a soy-wasabi dressing. The Asian noodle salad gets wrapped up in refreshing lettuce leaves along with seared tofu or shrimp and a spicy Thai dressing.

These salads are definitely lighter, fresher, and more seasonal that the usual bowl of mayonnaise-laden elbow noodles.

PASTA SALAD BASICS

148
·
RAISING
THE
SALAD
BAR
·

These hints will help you create unique and delicious pasta salads year-round.

Cooking Pasta for Pasta Salads

Add salt to the cooking water! Try at least 1 tablespoon or more of kosher salt per pot of water. The result won't be salty, just more flavorful. Cook the pasta until it is al dente, that is, with a slight bite, and drain it well. Add a tablespoon of olive oil to prevent the pasta from sticking together. Shake the strainer a few times to distribute the oil and let steam escape—this stops the cooking. You now have perfectly prepared pasta, ready to go.

Experiment with Different Kinds of Pasta

Small shapes like penne, bowtie, rotini, cavatappi or orzo make it easier to eat pasta salads and to hold dressings and herbs. Cheese-filled tortellini add heft. Large Israeli couscous and Italian couscous, which are tapioca-size, have a nice chewy texture and shape. Try Asian noodles like rice sticks and Japanese udon noodles. Whole wheat and flavored pastas are becoming more popular too. Start with 8 to 12 ounces for a typical pasta salad that serves 4 to 6.

Seasonal Vegetables

Good fresh vegetables for pasta salads include red onion, scallions, julienned carrots, cucumbers, tomatoes, red or yellow bell peppers, and micro- or baby greens like spinach, arugula, watercress and mizuna. Other additions, such as green beans, broccoli, cauliflower, zucchini, yellow squash, asparagus, corn and sugar snap peas need to be cooked until they're just crisp-tender. A quick sauté or a plunge into boiling water for 1 to 4 minutes turns the vegetables a vibrant color, and makes them easier to chew. (See the vegetable chapter, page 219, to learn about cooking times and methods for individual vegetables.) To stop the cooking and maintain color, immediately run vegetables under cold water after draining. Grilling or roasting vegetables also adds great flavor to pasta salads.

Tomatoes

Colorful, ripe tomatoes of all shapes and varieties can almost always be added to a pasta salad. They provide a flavorful and juicy contrast that boosts the flavor of the entire dish. Choose tomatoes at their peak of freshness, which will depend on the season. Sun-dried tomatoes, finely chopped, and cherry tomatoes are handy candidates when tomatoes are out of season.

Fresh Herbs and Cheeses

Fresh herbs almost always enhance a pasta salad, especially minced parsley. Also try chives, dill, fresh basil, mint and oregano.

In addition to the taste of fresh herbs, cheese can round out that last bit of flavor in a pasta salad. Creamy, tender, fresh mozzarella, shaved Italian Parmesan, ricotta salata, feta cheese, and blue cheeses are good starters to experiment with.

Dressings

Any of the dressings accompanying the pasta salad recipes in this chapter can be reworked into your own unique variations. The lemon dressings, herb vinaigrettes and the simple Greek vinegar and olive oil duo adapt to many pasta salads. The tomato and olive dressing packs some real punch and works well with chicken, broccoli, green beans and artichoke hearts, among other ingredients.

Serving and Presentation

Pasta salads taste best before they're refrigerated, or when they've been refrigerated for just a short time. Refrigerating pasta salads with tomatoes is not a good idea; tomatoes lose their flavor and become watery. To keep vegetables bright-looking and greens crisp, add the dressing just before serving. You can make the dressing and chop the herbs and vegetables ahead of time, and just prepare the pasta on the same day you plan to serve it. If the salad sits out for a while and the pasta absorbs the liquids, it might need more dressing, or a squeeze of lemon juice and a touch of olive oil to perk it up.

Instead of a deep bowl, use larger, shallow bowls or platters for serving. The glimpses of colorful vegetables and other additions are pretty and inviting.

SERVES 5 TO 6

TORTELLINI AND BABY SPINACH PASTA SALAD

Cheese-filled tortellini makes a substantial salad, and the Tomato-Olive Vinaigrette gives it a bit of zing.

1 pound fresh or frozen cheese tortellini
6 to 8 ounces baby spinach, roughly chopped
2 cups diced cooked chicken
Parmigiano Reggiano cheese, for garnish

TOMATO-OLIVE VINAIGRETTE
2 tablespoon red wine vinegar
2 tablespoons fresh lemon juice
1/2 teaspoon minced garlic
2/3 cup olive oil
1/2 cup seeded tomatoes, cut into 1/4-inch dice
3 tablespoons chopped kalamata olives
1 tablespoon minced fresh parsley
Salt and pepper

1 Bring a large pot of salted water to boil and cook the tortellini according to package directions. Drain the pasta, and immediately combine it with the spinach in a large bowl, so that the spinach wilts slightly. Gently mix several times.

2 To make the dressing, in a medium bowl, combine the vinegar, lemon juice and garlic. Slowly whisk in the oil. Stir in the chopped tomatoes, olives, parsley and salt and pepper. To the pasta, add the chicken and 1/2 cup of the dressing, spooning up a lot of tomatoes and olives. Mix well and add more dressing if needed.

3 When ready to serve, transfer the salad to a platter. Garnish with shaved Parmesan cheese.

COUSCOUS SALAD WITH ROASTED VEGETABLES

Large couscous is a pasta that's shaped like tapioca pearls. It is usually labeled Israeli couscous, or Italian couscous, if it's toasted. Either one, combined with oven-roasted vegetables, makes a refreshingly new, versatile side dish to accompany a main course. Couscous tastes best served at room temperature on the same day it's made. In the winter, serve this just after the vegetables are roasted and are still warm. Dice all of the vegetables approximately the same size—about 1/2 inch.

1 medium zucchini, diced
1 medium yellow squash, diced
1 red bell pepper, cored and diced
1 yellow bell pepper, cored and diced
1/2 red onion, diced
2 cloves garlic, halved lengthwise (do not peel)
3 tablespoons olive oil
Salt and pepper
1/2 pound Italian or Israeli couscous
2 tablespoons minced parsley

DRESSING
Grated zest of 1 lemon
2 tablespoons fresh lemon juice
1 tablespoon olive oil
Salt and pepper

1 Preheat the oven to 375°. Divide the zucchini, yellow squash, bell peppers, red onion and garlic cloves between two baking sheets (don't crowd the vegetables or they will steam instead of roast) and drizzle with 2 tablespoons of the oil. Mix well. Season with salt, and bake until vegetables are tender and beginning to brown, about 25 to 30 minutes.

2 Meanwhile, cook the large couscous in a large pot of boiling salted water, according to package instructions. Drain well and add 1 tablespoon of the oil. Shake strainer to incorporate oil and let couscous cool.

3 Remove the roasted garlic cloves from the baking sheet and remove their skins. In a small bowl, mash the garlic with a fork. Add the dressing ingredients: lemon zest, lemon juice, 1 tablespoon oil, and salt and pepper. Transfer pasta to a large serving bowl or platter and mix with the dressing. Stir in the vegetables and parsley, and adjust the seasonings if necessary.

VARIATIONS For eggplant lovers, add a small eggplant, peeled and diced the same size as the other vegetables, and use a bit more olive oil for roasting. Other good additions include chickpeas, cubed feta cheese, baby spinach and pine nuts.

LEMONY ASPARAGUS AND ARTICHOKE PASTA SALAD

Elegant and delicious, this salad will win raves. The method for roasting canned artichoke hearts to rekindle their flavor was suggested by a chef and friend, Tina Miller. This salad tastes and looks best on the day it's made.

1 can (14 ounces) artichoke hearts
1 tablespoon fresh lemon juice
3 tablespoons olive oil
1 clove garlic, minced
1/2 pound bowtie pasta
1 pound asparagus, bottom 2 inches trimmed, cut into 1 & 1/2-inch pieces
1 cup watercress, washed, dried, and roughly chopped, or 1/3 cup minced parsley
1 cup feta cheese, diced

LEMON DRESSING
Grated zest of 2 lemons
3 tablespoons lemon juice
2 tablespoons olive oil
1/2 teaspoon kosher salt
Pepper

1 Preheat the oven to 400°. Drain the artichokes, rinse well and cut them into quarters. Pat dry with paper towels and place on a parchment-lined baking sheet. Toss the artichokes with the lemon juice, 1 tablespoon of the oil, and minced garlic; bake until edges begin to crisp, about 15 to 20 minutes.

2 Meanwhile, bring a large pot of salted water to a boil and cook pasta until al dente, according to package directions. Drain the pasta and drizzle with 1 tablespoon of the oil. Shake strainer a few times to distribute the oil and let steam escape. Set aside to cool.

3 Heat a heavy skillet or cast iron pan over medium-high heat. Add the remaining tablespoon olive oil and the asparagus pieces. Cook asparagus until just crisp-tender, about 4 minutes, stirring often. Place in a bowl to cool.

4 When the pasta and asparagus are cool, combine them with the watercress or parsley in a large bowl. To make the dressing, in a small bowl, whisk together the lemon zest, lemon juice and oil. Season with salt and pepper. Just before serving, add dressing to the pasta and mix. Stir in the artichokes, gently fold in the feta, and transfer the salad to a serving dish.

SERVES 6

JAPANESE NOODLE SALAD WITH GINGER-SOY VINAIGRETTE

Japanese udon noodles, which are about the same width as fettuccine, have a smooth but firm texture that makes them an interesting match with vegetables…and this salad has plenty, plus a bright ginger-soy dressing. Udon can usually be found in the Asian section of your supermarket. I prefer the wheat udon noodles, which hold up well in a salad, but other pastas will also work.

1 package (8 ounces) dried udon noodles
1 tablespoon toasted sesame oil
4 stalks bok choy (with green tops), cut in half lengthwise and thinly sliced
1 celery stalk, peeled, cut in half lengthwise, and thinly sliced
1 carrot, cut into matchsticks
1 red bell pepper, cored and julienned
4 scallion greens, thinly sliced
2 tablespoons toasted sesame seeds

GINGER-SOY VINAIGRETTE
2 tablespoons soy sauce
1 tablespoon fresh lemon juice
2 teaspoons finely grated fresh ginger
2 tablespoons canola or peanut oil
1 tablespoon toasted sesame oil

1 Bring a large pot of salted water to a boil. Break the udon noodles in half and cook according to package directions (use the lesser amount of time indicated). Drain the noodles and add the sesame oil. Shake strainer several times to distribute the oil and release steam until noodles are cool.

2 In a large serving bowl, toss the vegetables with the udon noodles.

3 To make the dressing, in a small bowl, whisk together the soy sauce, lemon juice, ginger and both oils. Just before serving, add the dressing to the salad and mix well. Garnish with sesame seeds.

PESTO PASTA SALAD WITH CHICKEN AND OVEN-ROASTED TOMATOES

Oven-roasting tomatoes is an easy technique that intensifies their flavor. In this recipe you can roast them at the same time you roast the chicken. If good, fresh tomatoes are out of season, substitute rehydrated sun-dried tomatoes or deli-roasted tomatoes with herbs.

2 split, bone-in chicken breasts (with skin), or 2 cups cooked, shredded chicken
2 tablespoons olive oil
Salt and pepper
1 pint cherry or plum tomatoes, halved
Pinch of sugar
1/2 pound penne or spiral-shaped pasta
Pine nuts, for garnish
Torn basil leaves, for garnish

BASIL-PARSLEY PESTO
2 cups fresh basil leaves
1/2 cup fresh parsley
2 cloves garlic
1/3 cup grated Parmigiano Reggiano cheese
1/2 cup olive oil
Salt

1 Preheat the oven to 350°. Rub split chicken breasts with a little olive oil and season on both sides with salt. Place on a baking sheet and roast for 35 to 40 minutes, until just cooked. When chicken is cool enough to handle, remove the meat from the bone and shred by hand into thin strips. Refrigerate, covered, until ready to use.

2 While the chicken is roasting, place the tomato halves cut side up on a baking sheet lined with parchment paper. Drizzle with 1 tablespoon of the oil and season with salt and a pinch or two of sugar. Roast tomatoes for about 15 minutes; set aside to cool.

3 In a large pot of boiling, salted water, cook the pasta according to package directions until it is al dente. Drain well and add a splash of oil. Shake the strainer a few times to distribute the oil and stop the cooking.

4 To make the pesto, in a food processor combine the basil, parsley and garlic; process until mixture is coarsely chopped. Add the cheese, oil and salt and process until pesto is smooth.

5 Toss pasta with enough pesto to evenly coat. Season the reserved chicken with salt and pepper, and combine with pasta. Top with roasted tomatoes, pine nuts and basil.

VARIATIONS Add 1 cup steamed green beans, or broccoli florets to the pasta salad before tossing with the pesto.

SERVES 10 TO 12

SUMMER PASTA SALAD WITH TOMATO, FRESH MOZZARELLA, CORN AND BASIL

A great summer pasta dish with a winning combination of seasonal ingredients. It goes with just about everything and all ages love it. Dress this salad just before serving. I usually cut and add the basil at the last minute to keep it from turning.

1 pound penne
Kernels from 3 ears of corn
  (about 1 & 1/2 cups)
1 tablespoon olive oil
1 & 1/2 cups fresh mozzarella, cut into
  small cubes
3 or 4 tomatoes, cored and diced
Grated zest of 1 lemon
1 cup fresh basil leaves

DRESSING
3 tablespoons fresh lemon juice
1 tablespoon red wine vinegar
1 teaspoon finely minced garlic
1/3 cup olive oil
1/2 teaspoon kosher salt

1 Bring a large pot of salted water to a boil and add the pasta. About 2 minutes before pasta finishes cooking, add the corn kernels. Continue cooking until pasta is al dente and corn is just crisp-tender. Drain the corn and pasta and add the oil to keep pasta from sticking together. Shake the strainer to distribute the oil and stop the cooking. Let cool.

2 In a large serving bowl, toss the pasta and corn with fresh mozzarella, tomatoes and lemon zest.

3 To make the dressing, in a small bowl, whisk together all of the dressing ingredients. Just before serving, dress the salad, then slice the basil leaves into thin strips and gently stir them in.

PASTA SALAD WITH CHICKEN, ARTICHOKES AND SUN-DRIED TOMATO

A little shaved Parmesan or fresh mozzarella would be a nice addition to this satisfying, multi-textured dish. Serve along with some grilled garlic bread.

1/2 pound penne or spiral-shaped pasta
1/2 cup sun-dried tomatoes
Olive oil
2 boneless, skinless chicken breast cutlets (about 1 pound), butterflied
Salt and pepper
1 can (14 ounces) artichoke hearts, rinsed and quartered
1 endive, cored and cut into thin strips, or 1 cup micro-greens or chopped frisée
1/4 cup Greek or French olives, pitted and chopped
1/4 cup lightly packed minced parsley

1 Bring a large pot of salted water to a boil and cook pasta until al dente. In a small bowl, re-hydrate the sun-dried tomatoes by covering them with some of the boiling pasta water. Drain pasta, add a splash of olive oil to keep it from sticking, and shake the colander a few times to release steam and stop the cooking. When the sun-dried tomatoes have soaked for at least 10 minutes, drain them well and finely chop.

2 Season the chicken with salt and pepper. Heat a heavy-bottomed skillet over medium-high heat until hot. Add olive oil to coat the pan. Sauté cutlets and tenderloins, without moving them, until lightly browned on the first side, about 3 to 5 minutes. Turn and cook until second side is lightly browned, another 3 to 4 minutes. Let cool, then cut into 1/2-inch dice.

3 On a large serving platter, combine the cooled pasta, chicken, artichokes, endive or other greens, sun-dried tomatoes, olives and parsley.

4 To make the dressing, in a small bowl, whisk together the dressing ingredients; generously season with salt and pepper and toss with the pasta salad. Taste, and adjust the seasonings if necessary.

VARIATIONS Substitute broccoli that has been steamed for 3 minutes for the artichoke hearts. If you've grilled the chicken instead of pan-searing it, also grill some peeled eggplant slices and use in place of artichoke hearts. Or leave out the chicken entirely and substitute all grilled or roasted vegetables such as zucchini, yellow squash and eggplant for a completely vegetarian dish.

DRESSING
2 tablespoons red wine vinegar
2 teaspoons fresh lemon juice
1 clove garlic, finely minced
1 teaspoon dried oregano
6 tablespoons olive oil
Salt and pepper

SERVES 6

161
·
RAISING
THE
SALAD
BAR
·

EDAMAME, SHRIMP AND SNOW PEA PASTA SALAD

This is a good "go-to" recipe when you need a nutritious, delicious, pretty salad for any occasion. Don't skip the wasabi in the dressing; it adds a lot of flavor. Look for Japanese udon noodles in the Asian section of your supermarket, or substitute another pasta you like.

1 package (8 ounces) dried udon noodles

1 tablespoon toasted sesame oil

1 cup edamame beans, fresh or frozen

1 cup snow peas, strings removed

Olive oil

1 pound small to medium shrimp, peeled and deveined

Salt and pepper

1 large clove garlic, finely minced

1 red bell pepper, cored and cut into thin strips

1/4 cup thinly sliced scallion greens

1/2 cup unsalted, dry roasted peanuts

WASABI-SOY VINAIGRETTE

4 teaspoons wasabi powder

1/4 cup fresh lemon juice

2 tablespoons soy sauce

5 tablespoons canola or grapeseed oil

1 Break the udon noodles in half and cook in boiling salted water, according to package directions (use the lesser amount of time indicated). Drain noodles well, drizzle sesame oil over them and shake strainer occasionally to help release steam and stop the cooking. Let cool.

2 Bring a small pot of water to a boil and add the edamame beans. Cook for about 3 minutes, then add the snow peas. Cook 1 minute more. Drain the beans and pea pods and run them under cold water to stop the cooking.

3 Heat a large sauté pan over medium-high heat. Coat with a little oil, add the shrimp and sauté. Season shrimp with salt and pepper, and after about 3 minutes, add the minced garlic. Continue cooking shrimp until they turn pink, another 1 or 2 minutes, turning them once.

4 In a large serving bowl, combine the shrimp with the noodles, snow peas, edamame, red pepper and scallions.

5 To make the dressing, in a small bowl, mix the wasabi powder with 2 teaspoons water. Stir to form a paste and then stir in the lemon juice, soy sauce and canola or grapeseed oil. Just before serving, dress the salad and toss to combine. Garnish with peanuts.

WASABI Wasabi powder mixed with water makes the spicy wasabi paste we enjoy with sushi. When it's added to a dressing, the wasabi mellows quite a bit yet still adds a tasty little jolt. Look for wasabi powder that has real wasabi as an ingredient; some do not.

SERVES 6

GREEK PASTA SALAD WITH TOMATO, CUCUMBER, OLIVES AND FETA CHEESE

If you like Greek salads, you'll love this pasta salad full of vegetables, herbs, olives and feta cheese. You can also add chickpeas, artichokes, baby greens, chicken, homemade garlic croutons (page 23), or fresh seafood such as shrimp or calamari. For a crowd, just double the recipe.

1/2 pound fusilli pasta
1 tablespoon olive oil
1/2 pound tomatoes, seeded and diced
1 cucumber, peeled, seeded and diced
1/2 cup diced, pitted kalamata olives
1/4 red onion, sliced razor thin
1/4 cup packed minced fresh parsley
1 cup diced feta cheese

HERB DRESSING
1/4 cup red wine vinegar
3/4 cup olive oil
1/2 cup minced fresh basil, oregano and/or dill
1 teaspoon finely minced garlic
Salt and pepper

1 Bring a large pot of salted water to a boil. Cook pasta until al dente, according to package directions, then drain well in a colander and drizzle with 1 tablespoon olive oil. Shake the strainer to distribute oil and let steam escape. Set aside to cool.

2 When the pasta is cool, place it in a serving bowl and add the tomatoes, cucumber, olives, red onion and parsley.

3 To make the dressing, in a jar with a lid, combine the vinegar, oil, herbs and garlic. Season generously with salt and pepper. Shake well until the ingredients are emulsified and add 1/3 to 1/2 cup of the dressing to the salad just before serving. (Reserve leftover dressing for another salad.) Taste and make any necessary seasoning adjustments. Gently fold in the feta.

SPICY THAI LETTUCE WRAPS

Wrap this refreshing mix of noodles, tofu and vegetables in lettuce leaves and eat them with your fingers. This is a great way to serve tofu; but the dish works equally well with cooked shrimp. I often serve both to offer a choice. These wraps can be served as a first course (like a salad course) or as a main meal with soup. They're a lot of fun.

1 pound extra-firm tofu
1/3 cup flour
1 teaspoon curry powder
Canola oil
6 ounces rice vermicelli
3 cups Napa cabbage
1 carrot, peeled and julienned or shredded
4 scallion greens, sliced
1/2 cup slivered fresh mint leaves
1/4 cup chopped fresh cilantro leaves
1 or 2 heads butterhead or leafy lettuce

1 Wrap the tofu in a clean kitchen towel, or in several layers of paper towels, and let it rest for 10 minutes (the towel absorbs excess moisture from the tofu). Cut tofu crosswise into 8 pieces, then cut each of them into 4 pieces. Place the flour on a plate, mix in the curry powder and dredge tofu pieces on all sides.

2 Heat a large sauté pan and add enough canola oil to lightly coat the bottom. When the oil is hot enough for a piece of the tofu to sizzle, add as many pieces as the pan can hold without crowding. Cook until one side is golden, about 5 to 8 minutes. Carefully turn pieces of tofu over and cook on the other side until golden.

3 Bring a large pot of water to a boil. Add the rice noodles and cook until they're tender, about 4 or 5 minutes, then drain and rinse under cold water.

4 Thinly slice the Napa cabbage and place in a bowl. Add the carrot, scallions, mint and cilantro, and toss well to evenly distribute the ingredients.

CONTINUED ON NEXT PAGE

SPICY THAI LETTUCE WRAPS

THAI DRESSING
6 tablespoons lime juice
2 tablespoons sugar
3 tablespoons Asian fish sauce
1/2 teaspoon minced garlic
1/2 teaspoon red pepper flakes

5 To make the dressing, in a small bowl, combine all of the dressing ingredients.

6 Wash and spin dry whole lettuce leaves. Place them around the edges of a large serving platter. Place the noodles at one end of the patter, the Napa cabbage mixture in the center, and the tofu at the opposite end. Present the platter with 2 bowls of the dressing.

7 To eat the salad, place a few of the noodles, some of the cabbage mixture and a few pieces of tofu onto a lettuce leaf. Add a spoonful or two of dressing, fold over the sides of the lettuce leaf and roll up, wrap-style. Eat with your fingers.

VARIATION To make shrimp wraps, purchase 1 pound of small to medium shrimp. Peel and devein them, and sauté in 1 tablespoon of peanut or olive oil. Halfway through cooking, add 1 minced clove of garlic, and salt and pepper. Sauté shrimp until they're pink and cooked through, about 4 or 5 minutes, turning them once. You can also substitute or add seared fresh tuna.

BIG
BEAUTIFUL
BEAN
SALADS

BIG BEAUTIFUL BEAN SALADS

Beans make sensational salads and offer a change from leafy green, pasta or potato salads. Colorful and appealing, bean salads readily adapt to vibrant flavor combinations from different cuisines including Southwestern, Thai, Asian, Mediterranean, Latin American, Middle Eastern and Indian.

Beans—and therefore bean salads—are stocked with protein, calcium, iron and fiber, plus additional nutrients from the fruit, vegetables and greens you add to the mix. Black beans, pinto beans and kidney beans are among the top 20 foods that are highest in antioxidants, right up there with other antioxidant-rich foods like blueberries and cranberries. Beans are a staple food in much of the world, and as one food writer has noted, three-quarters of the world can't be wrong.

The first question I'm almost always asked is, "Can I use canned beans?" It's certainly easy to open a can, and the texture of canned beans is often pretty good. Adding a vinaigrette usually brightens their flavors and diminishes taste differences, as long as the beans are rinsed well.

But it's also easy to cook dried beans—about as easy as boiling water. You can cook them while you're watching TV, answering e-mail or paying bills. The reward is a good, clean taste, ready to be enhanced with flavorings. It's a shame that beans are so overlooked in today's world of food shortcuts. This is my small chapter dedicated to keeping alive a food that's definitely worth enjoying.

While canned beans are a fine substitute, home-cooked beans have better flavor and texture.

Preparing

Carefully inspect dry beans, removing any small stones or clumps of grit; then rinse beans under cold water.

Soaking

Place beans in a bowl or pot, amply cover with water, and let soak overnight, uncovered. Soaking the beans decreases their cooking time and eliminates some of their gas-producing sugars. When ready to cook beans, drain them well and discard the soaking water.

Quick-Soaking

If you forget to soak beans overnight, use a "quick-soak" method: Put beans in a large saucepan or pot and cover with 2 to 3 inches of water. Bring to a boil, turn off heat, and let beans soak in the hot water, covered, for 1 hour. They will absorb water and expand. Drain well.

Cooking

Place soaked beans in a large pot, and cover them with at least 3 or 4 inches of fresh, cold water. Bring to a boil, reduce heat to a simmer, partially cover, and cook until beans are soft and cooked through, but not falling apart. The average time for most beans is about 1 to 1 & 1/2 hours (chickpeas take the longest). It's best to add salt after beans are almost entirely cooked. When the beans are done, either drain them in a colander or leave them in the cooking water until they're cool; then drain.

When cooking beans, make sure they are thoroughly cooked, that is, tender, but not mushy. This can be achieved by testing the beans periodically; remove one or two beans and press them between your thumb and index finger. With pressure, the beans should squish when done. Undercooked beans won't absorb flavors well, and they're unpleasant to eat.

BEAN SALAD BASICS

Experiment with Different Types of Beans

These bean varieties work well in salads: black, pinto, kidney, white beans such as cannellini or navy, black-eyed peas and chickpeas. The French green lentils (sometimes labeled "du Puy") hold their shape best in lentil salads. Try heirloom beans, older varieties that are coming back on the market.

Avoid Buying Old Beans

Even though beans are dried and seem to last forever, they do taste best when used within a year of harvesting. I was amazed once when I cooked dried kidney beans that had been grown in someone's garden. The beans were perfectly creamy without as much as a crack when cooked, and they were full-flavored. In supermarkets, look for uniformly sized, brightly colored beans. Avoid buying cracked or broken beans—these are signs of old age. Also avoid preparing mixed batches of different beans because cooking times will vary for each.

Think Color

Add colorful vegetables and fruit to beans for contrast and variety. Corn kernels, red and yellow bell peppers, chopped scallions, green beans, shredded carrots, red onion, parsley and cilantro almost always work well in bean salads. Mix in leafy greens like watercress, mizuna or frisée. Some fruits, such as mango, orange and pineapple taste good and add plenty of bright color.

Increase Amounts of Vinegar or Citrus Used in Dressings

Equal parts of vinegar or citrus to olive oil usually does the trick for bean salads, or 1 tablespoon vinegar or citrus juice to 1 or 2 tablespoons oil. Bean salads taste fresh and vibrant with all kinds of fresh citrus juices, including lemon, lime or orange juice. The individual dressings in these recipes can generally be interchanged and used to make your own bean salads.

Serve at Room Temperature, Dressed on the Same Day

Salad components can be made ahead of time, especially cooking the beans. If serving leftovers, it's best to bring them to room temperature and add another shot of lime or lemon juice and some olive oil to replace liquid that has been absorbed.

Great Flavoring Tip

My favorite tip for flavoring beans as they cook is to add one or two dried chipotle peppers, which are smoked jalapeño peppers (do not use canned chipotles in adobo sauce) as they cook. Chipotles impart a subtle smoky flavor to the beans as they cook. I discard the pepper afterward, or occasionally blend a portion of it into the dressing for a touch of heat. This method works best for pinto, kidney and black beans. You will find dried chipotle peppers in most supermarkets, Latin American markets, or from online sources.

EDAMAME, CORN AND BEAN SALAD

I had been looking for a way to use the fresh green soybeans, known as edamame, found at New England farmers markets in late August. (They can also be found frozen in the supermarket year round.) I finally hit upon this winning combination of fresh edamame, sweet summer corn and meaty red kidney beans, dressed with a salsa-inspired dressing. It's really simple to make, and loaded with protein, calcium, iron and fiber. This salad can double as a colorful dip.

1 pint fresh edamame pods or 1 cup shelled edamame beans

Kernels from 3 ears fresh corn (about 2 cups)

1 cup cooked kidney beans, or from 1 can (15 ounces), rinsed and drained

1/3 cup chopped fresh cilantro

SALSA DRESSING

2 tomatoes, seeded and finely diced (about 1 cup)

2 tablespoons minced red onion

1 teaspoon ground cumin

3 tablespoons fresh lime juice

2 tablespoons olive oil

Salt

1 In a medium saucepan, bring 6 to 8 cups of water to a boil and cook the edamame pods for about 10 minutes. If using frozen beans, follow package instructions. Drain, rinse under cold water and remove the beans from their pods (discard pods). You should have about 1 cup of beans. Steam the corn kernels for 3 minutes; set aside. In a serving bowl, combine the edamame beans, corn and kidney beans.

2 To make the dressing, in a small bowl, combine the tomato, red onion, cumin, lime juice, olive oil and salt. Stir to combine. To taste the dressing for seasoning, combine a small amount of the salad and the dressing. If necessary, make any adjustments, such as adding more citrus or salt.

3 When ready to serve, add the dressing to the salad. Dress only the amount of salad you think you will serve that day. Mix in the chopped cilantro. This salad tastes best at room temperature. If it sits for a while or is stored in the refrigerator, perk it up with some more lime juice.

VARIATIONS Try different dressings, such as a Fresh Herb Vinaigrette (page 250) or Cilantro-Lime Vinaigrette (page 252). You can also add minced garlic or hot chiles to the Salsa Dressing. Mix in some cottage cheese for lunch. You can also make this salad with just the corn and edamame.

SERVES 6 TO 8

174
·
RAISING
THE
SALAD
BAR
·

CHICKPEA, WATERCRESS AND MANGO SALAD WITH LIME-CURRY VINAIGRETTE

In this salad, the tropical flavors of mango, curry and lime are perfect matches for the creamy, mild-tasting chickpeas. The addition of watercress and red bell pepper makes this a colorful and nutritious salad, that tastes best at room temperature on the day it's made.

1 & 1/2 cups cooked chickpeas, or 1 can (14 ounces) chickpeas, rinsed

1 roasted red bell pepper, diced

1 mango, peeled and cut into 1/2-inch dice

1 cucumber, peeled, halved, seeded and cut into 1/2-inch dice

1 bunch watercress (about 2 cups), washed and dried, large stems removed, roughly chopped

LIME-CURRY VINAIGRETTE

2 & 1/2 tablespoons fresh lime juice

1 & 1/2 teaspoons curry powder

1 teaspoon minced fresh ginger

1 teaspoon honey or brown sugar

4 tablespoons canola oil

Salt and pepper

1 In a large bowl, combine the chickpeas, roasted red pepper, mango and cucumber.

2 To make the dressing, in a medium bowl, whisk together the lime juice, curry powder, ginger, honey or brown sugar, oil, salt and pepper. When ready to serve, add dressing only to the amount of salad you think you will serve that day. Add the watercress and dressing to the chickpea mixture and toss to combine. Store remaining salad and dressing separately, covered, in the refrigerator.

VARIATION You can make this a black bean and mango salad by substituting black beans for the chickpeas, and 1 teaspoon each of cumin and coriander for the curry powder in the dressing.

SERVES 6 TO 8

175
·
RAISING
THE
SALAD
BAR
·

BLACK BEAN, CORN AND RED PEPPER SALAD WITH CHILE-LIME DRESSING

Here's a vibrant, colorful salad with many uses: a side dish, a topping for fish or chicken, or as a dip with chips.

1 & 1/4 cups dried black beans, soaked overnight, or 2 cans (15 ounces each) black beans

Kernels from 2 ears fresh corn, about 2 cups

1 red bell pepper, roasted or raw, diced

3 scallion greens, very thinly sliced

1/4 cup minced red onion

1/4 cup chopped fresh cilantro

CHILI-LIME DRESSING

1/2 teaspoon ground cumin

1/2 teaspoon chile powder

Pinch of cayenne or ground chipotle pepper

6 tablespoons fresh lime juice

5 tablespoons olive oil

1/2 teaspoon kosher salt, or to taste

1 In a large saucepan, cover the soaked, drained beans with 2 inches of water and bring to a boil. Reduce heat and simmer, partially covered, until beans are cooked through but still whole, about 50 to 60 minutes. Drain and let cool. If using canned beans, drain and rinse well. Steam the corn kernels for 3 minutes; set aside to cool.

2 In a medium bowl, combine the beans, corn, red pepper, scallions and red onion.

3 To make the dressing, in a separate bowl, whisk together the spices, lime juice, oil and salt. Add to salad and mix well. Just before serving, add the cilantro.

SERVES 6 TO 8

BOUNTIFUL ITALIAN BEAN SALAD

After eating winter green beans that are bright green and unblemished, but have little flavor, I look forward to the local summer crop. The green beans or haricots verts I find at the farmers market are so slender, and so tasty, they are great in any salad. If wax beans are unavailable, double the amount of green beans.

1 & 1/2 cups haricots verts (slender French green beans), trimmed and cut in half

1 & 1/2 cups wax beans, trimmed and cut in halves or thirds

1 & 1/2 cups cooked chickpeas, or 1 can (14 ounces) chickpeas, rinsed

1 & 1/2 cups cooked kidney beans, or 1 can (14 ounces) kidney beans, rinsed

1 roasted red bell pepper, diced

1/4 cup chopped scallion greens or minced parsley

LEMON-LIME DRESSING

2 tablespoons fresh lemon juice

1 tablespoon fresh lime juice

1/2 teaspoon finely minced garlic

1 teaspoon ground cumin

1/4 teaspoon red pepper flakes

6 tablespoons olive oil

1/2 teaspoon kosher salt, or more to taste

Pepper

1 Steam the green and wax beans separately until just crisp-tender, about 4 or 5 minutes for green beans; a little longer for the wax beans. Immediately run them under cold water to stop the cooking. In a large bowl, combine the green beans and wax beans, chickpeas, kidney beans, roasted pepper and scallions or parsley.

2 To make the dressing, in a small bowl, whisk together the lemon and lime juices, garlic, cumin, red pepper flakes, oil, salt and pepper to taste.

3 This salad tastes best at room temperature, on the day it's made. When ready to serve, dress only the amount of salad you think will be eaten that day. If it sits out for a while or is stored in the refrigerator, perk it up with more citrus juice. Store remaining salad and dressing separately, covered, in the refrigerator.

SERVES 6 TO 8

179
·
RAISING
THE
SALAD
BAR
·

LENTIL SALAD WITH MAPLE-BALSAMIC VINAIGRETTE

Of the many varieties of lentils, the small, mottled slate-green French lentils (also known as lentilles de Puy) hold their shape best when cooked and are perfect for this earthy, colorful salad. Because these lentils only take about 20 minutes to cook, this is an easy salad to put together and goes with just about everything. The lentils do not need to be soaked ahead of time.

1 & 1/2 cups French green lentils (de Puy), checked for stones and rinsed
1 bay leaf
Salt
1 carrot, peeled and shredded
1 red bell pepper, cored and finely diced
1/4 cup chopped scallion greens or minced parsley
1/2 cup raisins, roughly chopped
1 cup walnuts, toasted and chopped

MAPLE-BALSAMIC VINAIGRETTE
3 tablespoons balsamic vinegar
1 tablespoon fresh lemon juice
1 tablespoon maple syrup
1/4 cup olive oil
3/4 teaspoon kosher salt
Pepper

1 Fill a large saucepan with water, add the lentils and bay leaf; bring to a boil. Reduce heat and simmer, partially covered, until lentils are cooked, about 18 to 20 minutes. The lentils should be tender, but still holding their shape (not mushy). Drain lentils well, add a few pinches of salt and shake a few times as they cool to release steam.

2 When cool, combine the lentils, carrot, red bell pepper, scallions or parsley, and raisins in a serving bowl.

3 To make the dressing, in a separate bowl, whisk together the vinegar, lemon juice, maple syrup, olive oil, salt and pepper. This salad tastes best at room temperature on the day it's made. When ready to serve, add the dressing to the salad and mix well. Garnish with chopped walnuts.

VARIATIONS Add some cooked chickpeas. Or give the salad a Middle Eastern twist by reducing the maple syrup and balsamic vinegar, and adding more lemon juice, plus ground cumin and coriander, and either minced parsley or cilantro to taste.

SERVES 6 TO 8

180
·
RAISING
THE
SALAD
BAR
·

WHITE BEAN AND ASPARAGUS SALAD

I'm always looking for new ways to use the abundance of fresh asparagus that's available when it's in season. It can be served as a salad or first course, as a side dish or as a base for fish. You can simply add cooked shrimp, salmon or canned or fresh-seared tuna to make an entire, balanced meal.

1 & 1/2 cups dried white beans, soaked overnight or 2 cans (14 ounces each) white beans

1 pound asparagus, bottoms trimmed, cut into 1/2-inch pieces

1 or 2 roasted red bell peppers, diced

HERB VINAIGRETTE

3/4 cup olive oil

1/4 cup red or white wine vinegar

1/3 cup minced fresh basil, parsley, dill or cilantro

1 tablespoon finely minced shallot

Salt and pepper

1 Place the beans in a medium saucepan and cover with at least 2 inches of water; bring to a boil. Reduce heat to medium-low and simmer the beans until they are tender, but not mushy, about 45 to 60 minutes. Drain beans and allow them to cool. If using canned beans, rinse well and drain.

2 In a medium sauté pan, bring 1 inch of water to a boil. Add the asparagus pieces, cover, and cook until they are tender but still crisp, about 2 to 3 minutes. Drain asparagus and immediately run under cold water or place in a bowl of ice water to stop the cooking, then drain again. In a serving bowl combine the cooked asparagus with the white beans and red peppers.

3 In a small bowl, whisk all of the ingredients for the vinaigrette. Taste and adjust the seasonings if necessary. Add enough of the vinaigrette to moisten the beans. Cover the remaining vinaigrette and refrigerate for use in another salad.

GOOD FOR YOU GRAINS

GOOD-FOR-YOU GRAINS

What you'll love about grain salads—along with being power-packed with nutrients and flavor—is the ease of making them. Cooking grains is as simple as boiling water. Once cooked, these grains mix with colorful fresh vegetables and herbs, fruits, nuts and leafy greens for a dish that's as easy to put together as a plain green salad. You'll also get the benefit of whole grains and vegetables all in one dish.

Most of us are familiar with the Middle Eastern grain salad known as tabouli, a preparation of bulgur wheat with parsley, mint, fresh tomatoes, olive oil and lemon. It's a good way to demonstrate how a grain, when combined with vegetables, results in a much more rewarding dish than its individual parts.

As refreshing and versatile as tabouli can be, it's not the only grain salad. This chapter introduces you to other grains that are perfect for salads—from light and delicate quinoa to earthy wild rice, and even the exotic "forbidden" black rice. Rice, barley and wheat berries, along with their heirloom relatives, spelt berries and farro, are also excellent salad choices. These grains have a nut-like, sweet taste with a satisfying, chewy texture.

The grains used with these recipes are mostly whole grains—the much talked about "new" carbs that can help boost health. Unlike refined grains, whole grains retain their bran and germ which pack fiber, B vitamins and minerals. They're also a great source of phytonutrients, antioxidants, vitamin E and protein. When the bran and germ are processed out of the grain, about 25 percent of its protein is lost, along with 17 key nutrients, according to the Whole Grains Council. The USDA dietary guidelines recommend 3 servings of whole grains a day—and a grain salad is an easy way to get them.

Your friends and family will love these grain salads, as I have discovered. Whenever I serve them, they're always a hit and quickly disappear. I think it's because these dishes are light, refreshing, healthful and a little unusual. For my son's 5th birthday party I served the Thai Quinoa Salad on page 190 prepared with a colorful combination of cucumber, red pepper, carrots, cilantro and mint, along with an Asian peanut chicken salad. With just these two salads prepped the day before, I fed the 20 or so adults and was later given the unofficial award for best food at a children's birthday party.

This chapter helps you get to know the grains that make good salads and explains how to cook them, followed by my favorite recipes. Today, many of these grains can be found at your supermarket. Most are available at organic markets, health food stores and specialty stores, as well as from some online sources.

THE GRAINS

186
·
RAISING
THE
SALAD
BAR
·

Wheat Berry, Spelt and Kamut

Wheat berries are whole wheat kernels that have not been milled, polished or heat-treated. Most people don't realize that you can take a wheat berry before it's ground into flour or sprouted for wheat grass juice, and cook it in water. From the size of a very plump rice grain, when cooked it becomes a perfectly round, toothsome grain about the size of a small pea—ideal for a salad. It's nutty and chewy, and it tops the charts for healthy eating. The two different types of wheat berry—soft spring or hard winter—can both be used.

Spelt and kamut are types of so-called "ancient wheats" now on the market. They, too, cook up like wheat berries, and can be used to make wonderful salads. Spelt berries taste mildly nutty, and are sometimes used as substitutes for people who are allergic to wheat. Once cooked, their oblong shape resembles a tiny brown football.

All three grains can be used interchangeably in a salad. I use exactly the same cooking method for all three. I simply put them in a pot of mildly boiling water and cook them until they're done. This can take 60 to 80 minutes, admittedly a drawback in today's fast-paced environment. Still, don't be discouraged from finding or cooking these grains for a salad—you won't be sorry.

While there are suggestions to soak these wheat berries overnight to help cut down on cooking time, I've found that the time saved isn't worth the extra step. But feel free to experiment.

Farro

This certified organic product comes from Italy, specifically the Mugello region of Tuscany. Farro is the world's original grain from which all others are derived, including rice, barley, wheat and rye. Because it is hard to grow, farro almost became extinct during the 1940s. However, it is now making a big comeback, especially in Italy where top restaurants feature it in soups and side dishes. It has a pleasant nuttiness and a hearty texture and is naturally high in fiber, protein, and B vitamins.

Cracked Wheat and Bulgur

The words cracked wheat and bulgur are often used interchangeably. Both derive from the whole wheat berry, but there is a difference. Cracked wheat is made from whole dried wheat berries that have simply been ground into coarse, medium and fine granulations. Cracked wheat must be cooked.

Bulgur, on the other hand, is made by steam cooking the wheat berries and then drying them. The dried wheat is then cracked into fine, medium or coarse granules. Because bulgur has already been cooked, you just need boiling water for it to soften and swell. This makes bulgur one of the quickest grains to cook for a salad—unless you are using an already cooked, leftover grain, which is also a good idea.

Any of the 3 gradations of bulgur—coarse, medium and fine—can be used for salads. Middle Eastern recipes often specify the fine grade for tabouli; I like the slightly coarser medium size.

Bulgur and cracked wheat are usually found in health food markets. If you want to find the different gradations, look for a Middle Eastern food market in your area. These markets also offer other wonderful ingredients to include in salads such as feta cheese and olives, and even more exotic, delicious items like pomegranate molasses and tamarind paste.

Rice

Leftover cooked rice works well as the base for quick salad, or you can cook some up specifically for this purpose. The hardest part is deciding which rice to use. The stickiness of short grain brown rice or Arborio rice, used for making risotto, makes them unsuitable for a grain salad. Long grain brown or white rice hold their shapes nicely. Basmati or jasmine rice, which can be slightly sticky, has a wonderful nuttiness that contributes a special flavor note to salads.

Rice works nicely in combination with lentils, chickpeas and other beans in a salad, or you can mix in cooked chicken, turkey, or ham. Add vegetables like shredded carrots, or diced multi-colored peppers, celery, scallions, or corn. In addition to using herbs to spice up my salads, I often use some sweet curry powder; to make an Asian rice salad, I use soy sauce, ginger and sesame oil.

Black Rice

This medium-size, aromatic Chinese rice is fairly new to American markets, but it's actually an ancient grain once eaten exclusively by the Emperors of China. It has a delicious nutty taste, soft texture and a rich deep purple color. In fact, the color alone makes it fun to use for grain salads, but its flavor is even better. It's not glutinous or rough, and it cooks in 30 minutes. Black rice has a high nutritional value and is especially rich in iron. Look for this exotic rice at natural foods markets or some online sources.

Wild Rice

Technically, wild rice is a grass seed, not a grain, but for our purposes, it doesn't matter. When cooked, it produces a nutty, rich flavor and hearty body that's perfect for grain salads. I mix it with roasted vegetables for a colorful presentation, or flavor it with curry for something different. Native to North America, wild rice tastes wonderful with another native food, cranberries, and is also a good partner for apples or citrus.

Nutritionally, wild rice has about twice the protein of other rice varieties and significant levels of B vitamins that benefit the nervous system. Pregnant women will be well supplied with all-important folacin after eating this grain.

Wild rice cooks in about 45 to 50 minutes. It costs more than most grains, but 1 cup raw rice yields 3 to 4 cups cooked rice. That's perfect for a salad for four.

Quinoa

Everyone who tries a quinoa salad loves it. Pronounced "keen-wa," this whole grain is light and fluffy with an "unsticky" texture and a slightly crunchy spiraling tail (actually an external germ) to complement its delicate flavor.

It cooks in only 15 minutes, another plus, and then it's ready for a wide range of flavorings. It's quite vibrant with Thai flavors of lime and cilantro, but goes equally well with a Southwest-style combination of corn, red bell pepper, chiles and cumin. I sometimes make a quinoa "tabouli" with parsley, tomato, lemon juice and olive oil. You can substitute quinoa in any salad calling for couscous, barley or rice.

This small tan-colored South American grain is the only grain that is a complete protein. It contains as much as four times the nutrition of brown rice with significant quantities of calcium, iron, B vitamins, fiber and protein. That may be one reason quinoa was called "the mother grain" by the Incas.

The key to cooking quinoa is using the right amount of water. Most recipes that call for 2 cups of water to 1 cup quinoa yield a mushy result that's unsuitable for a salad. If your pot has a tight-fitting lid that doesn't allow much steam to escape, use 1 & 1/2 cups water for 1 cup of the grain. If your pot allows some steam to escape, increase the amount to 1 & 2/3 cups of water.

Barley

Barley has a particularly tough hull that is difficult to remove without losing some of the healthful bran. Hulled barley, available at health food stores, retains more whole-grain nutrients, but takes longer to cook—over 1 & 1/4 hours. Milling the grain produces lightly pearled barley. Although the process causes barley to lose some of its nutrients, it is more easily cooked and digested. For salads, combine barley with carrots, corn or colored peppers and herbs like cilantro, parsley or dill. Also try leafy greens like baby spinach, watercress or mizuna.

These recipes are an at-a-glance guide for preparing grains for use in salads.

WHEAT BERRY, SPELT AND KAMUT

1 to 1 & 1/2 cups wheat berries, spelt berries or kamut, rinsed
Large pot containing at least 3 quarts of water
Salt

Put the berries in a large pot and add enough cold water to cover them by 5 to 6 inches. Bring water to a boil, lower heat to medium and keep the water at a rapid simmer or soft boil, partially covered, until berries are done, approximately 1 hour and 15 minutes. They will be soft and slightly chewy. Start testing after about 50 minutes for a 'reference point' of chewiness. Add a little salt to taste after about 45 minutes of cooking time. Once you've cooked and sampled the grain in a dish, judging its degree of doneness becomes easy. Drain well and let cool. This recipe yields about 2 & 1/2 to 3 cups cooked wheat berries, spelt berries, or kamut.

FARRO

1 cup farro, rinsed
2 quarts water
Salt

Place farro in a large pot, cover it with 2 quarts of water and add some salt. Bring water to a boil, reduce heat and simmer, uncovered, for about 30 to 35 minutes. Farro will have a similar texture to barley when it's done. Drain well and let cool completely. This recipe yields about 2 & 1/2 cups cooked farro.

BULGUR

1 cup bulgur
1 & 1/2 cups boiling water
Large pinch of salt

Place bulgur in a metal or glass bowl. Add a generous pinch of salt and the boiling water. Stir once or twice to incorporate the water and cover the bowl with a plate. Let rest for about 20 to 30 minutes, or until the water is absorbed. Fluff with a fork and let cool to room temperature before using in a salad. This recipe yields about 3 cups cooked bulgur.

LONG GRAIN BROWN RICE

1 cup long grain brown rice, rinsed and drained
2 cups water
1/2 teaspoon kosher salt

In a heavy 2-quart saucepan, bring water and salt to a boil over high heat. Stir in the rice. Return water to a boil, then reduce heat to low and simmer, covered, for 35 to 40 minutes. Turn off the heat and let the rice rest, covered, for 5 to 10 minutes. Fluff with a fork. 1 cup raw rice yields about 2 & 1/2 cups cooked rice.

BLACK RICE

1 cup black rice, rinsed
1 & 3/4 cups water
Pinch of salt

In a medium saucepan, combine the rice, water and salt. Bring the water to a boil over high heat; cover, reduce heat and simmer rice for 30 minutes. Remove from heat. Let the rice rest, covered, for a few minutes. Fluff rice with a fork and serve. 1 cup raw rice yields 3 cups cooked rice.

WILD RICE

1 cup wild rice
5 cups water

Place the rice in a mesh strainer and rinse it twice. Transfer to a saucepan, add the water and bring to a boil. Reduce heat to medium-low and simmer, covered, for about 50 minutes or until grains have slightly burst open. Test the rice by biting into a few grains. At this point they should not be fully opened. Turn off the heat and drain the excess water. Let the rice rest, covered, for 5 to 10 minutes to absorb any excess water. For use in a salad, let cool. Wild rice lasts for several days in the refrigerator and can be frozen.

BARLEY

1 cup pearled barley
2 quarts water
1/2 teaspoon kosher salt

In a large saucepan, bring the water, barley and salt to a boil over high heat. Reduce heat to a simmer and cook, uncovered, for approximately 40 minutes, or until barley is tender but still chewy. Rinse barley under cold running water until cool; drain well. 1 cup of raw barley yields about 3 cups of cooked barley.

QUINOA

1 cup quinoa
1 & 1/2 cups water
1/2 teaspoon kosher salt

Place the grain in a medium saucepan, fill with water, swish it around with your fingers, and then drain using a large, very fine-mesh strainer. Repeat a second time. When completely drained, add 1 & 1/2 cups water and the salt to the saucepan and bring to a boil. Reduce heat to low, and cook, covered, for 13 to 15 minutes, or until all of the water is absorbed. Turn off the heat and let quinoa rest about 5 or 10 minutes more. For use in a salad, cool the quinoa completely. This recipe yields about 3 cups cooked quinoa.

SERVES 6 TO 8

THAI QUINOA SALAD

Quinoa comes alive in a salad with crispy vegetables and piquant Thai flavorings. Serve this salad along with other Asian dishes, or make it a meal in itself by adding cooked shrimp, crab or lobster.

1 cup quinoa, rinsed

1/2 teaspoon kosher salt

1 red bell pepper, cored and cut into very thin strips

1 carrot, peeled, and shredded or julienned

1 small cucumber, peeled, seeded and sliced

1/3 cup chopped fresh mint

1/2 cup chopped fresh cilantro

THAI DRESSING

6 tablespoons fresh lime juice

1 tablespoon sugar

1 tablespoon Asian fish sauce

1/2 teaspoon red pepper flakes

1 Add quinoa, salt and 1 & 1/2 cups water to a saucepan. Bring to a boil and then reduce heat to low, cover, and cook for 13 to 15 minutes, until the water is absorbed. Turn off the heat and let the quinoa sit for 5 minutes. Set aside to cool completely.

2 In a large serving bowl, combine the quinoa, red bell pepper, carrot and cucumber and mix well.

3 To make the dressing, in a small bowl, whisk together the lime juice and sugar until sugar is dissolved. Stir in the fish sauce and red pepper flakes. Add the dressing to the salad and toss. Gently mix in the mint and cilantro. If you're not serving the salad the same day, store it and the dressing separately, covered, in the refrigerator.

VARIATION Try making quinoa "wraps" by using lettuce leaves to wrap quinoa and shrimp, lobster or crab. This salad also tastes delicious with tofu.

ASIAN FISH SAUCE Most stores now carry this integral Thai ingredient. Made from salted, fermented anchovies, fish sauce does not add a "fishy" taste to foods, but gives them a salty, complex flavor. The clear brown liquid comes in a small bottle, and costs only a few dollars.

SERVES 6 TO 8

191
•
RAISING
THE
SALAD
BAR
•

BLACK BEAN AND RICE SALAD WITH CHILE-LIME VINAIGRETTE

The classic combination of rice and beans makes a wonderful salad. I've substituted nutty-tasting long grain brown rice for white rice, and it tastes delicious. The slender, more elegant-looking brown rice is less sticky than the short grain version and is a better choice for rice salads.

3/4 cup dried black beans, soaked overnight, or 1 can (15 ounces) black beans

1 cup long grain brown rice (about 3 cups cooked)

1/4 teaspoon kosher salt

1 red bell pepper, raw or roasted, cored and diced

1/4 cup finely chopped red onion

1/2 cup chopped cilantro leaves

CHILE-LIME VINAIGRETTE

1/2 teaspoon ground cumin

1/2 teaspoon chili powder or ancho chile powder

Pinch of cayenne or ground chipotle pepper

6 tablespoons fresh lime juice

6 tablespoons olive oil

1/2 teaspoon kosher salt

1 If using dried black beans, place them in a large saucepan and cover with 2 to 3 inches of water; bring to a boil. Reduce heat to a simmer and cook the beans, partially covered, until they are cooked through, but still whole, about 60 to 75 minutes. Drain the beans and set aside. If using canned beans, rinse and drain them well. Meanwhile, in a separate saucepan, add rice and salt to 2 cups of water. Bring to a boil and then reduce heat to low, cover, and cook for 35 to 40 minutes. Remove from heat and let sit for 5 minutes. Set aside to cool completely.

2 In a large serving bowl, combine the beans and the rice; mix in the red pepper and red onion.

3 To make the dressing, in a small bowl, whisk together all of the dressing ingredients.

4 Combine black bean and rice mixture with the dressing. Add the cilantro and toss.

VARIATION Add kernels from two ears of fresh corn for additional color and crunch. Add diced cooked chicken or shrimp. Spice up the dressing by adding 1 minced garlic clove or minced jalapeño pepper, or both.

SERVES 6

NUTTY WILD RICE SALAD

This autumn-inspired salad has apples, dried cranberries and a super-easy dressing of sweet cider and a tart touch of lemon juice. Toasted nuts add crunch to the pleasantly chewy wild rice. Try any combination of hazelnuts, pecans, walnuts, pine nuts or sliced almonds. This dish is perfect alongside chicken, pork tenderloin or pork chops.

1 cup wild rice, rinsed
1/2 teaspoon kosher salt
1 tart apple, diced (sprinkle a few drops of lemon juice over apple to prevent discoloration)
3/4 cup dried cranberries
1/2 cup finely minced parsley
1 cup mixed toasted nuts

APPLE CIDER DRESSING
1/2 cup apple cider juice
Grated zest of 1 lemon
1 tablespoon fresh lemon juice
3 tablespoons olive oil
1/2 teaspoon kosher salt

1 Add rice, salt, and 3 & 1/2 cups water to a saucepan and bring to a boil. Reduce heat to low, cover, and cook until rice is done, about 50 minutes. Many of the grains will split, but the rice will still have a little bite. Drain any excess water, and set aside to cool completely.

2 Combine cooked wild rice with the apple, cranberries and parsley in a large serving bowl.

3 To make the dressing, combine all of the dressing ingredients and mix with the salad just before serving. Top with nuts.

SERVES 6

193
·
RAISING
THE
SALAD
BAR
·

BULGUR SALAD WITH APRICOT, RADICCHIO AND PARSLEY

This is a gorgeous-looking salad with ruby-red radicchio, parsley, and a hint of sweetness from dried apricots. Dried fig or date lovers can use those instead.

1 cup bulgur
Salt
1/2 small head radicchio, cored and thinly sliced (about 1 cup)
1/2 cup chopped dried apricots
1/2 cup minced parsley
1/2 cup walnuts, toasted and chopped

LEMON DRESSING
4 tablespoons fresh lemon juice
4 tablespoons olive oil
1 small clove garlic, minced
1 teaspoon sumac (optional)
1/2 teaspoon kosher salt

1 Place the bulgur in a bowl, add 1 & 1/4 cups boiling water and 2 generous pinches of salt. Cover with a plate and let sit for about 20 minutes until the water is absorbed. Remove the cover and set aside to cool completely.

2 Place the bulgur in a large serving bowl. Stir in the radicchio, apricots and parsley.

3 To make the dressing, in a small bowl, combine all of the dressing ingredients and add to the salad just a few minutes before serving. Stir in the walnuts. If the salad remains out or if you're serving leftovers the next day, you may need to refresh the mixture by adding a touch more lemon juice and olive oil.

SUMAC A staple spice in the Middle East, reddish-colored ground sumac has a fruity sourness similar to that of lemons, though not as sharp. It's made from sumac berries that are sun-dried, then ground to a powder, and can be found in Middle Eastern grocery shops or some online sources.

WHEAT BERRY SALAD WITH CITRUS DRESSING

Wheat berries—also called whole grain wheat—are the kernels of whole wheat, unprocessed, with both the germ and bran intact. These provide essential nutritents, including protein, fiber, B vitamins, iron, calcium, folic acid, magnesium and other minerals. Many people are not aware that these berries can be cooked and used in various dishes. They make especially wonderful grain salads—chewy and satisfying. This is one of my favorites, with a light, citrusy dressing, dark green watercress and tart dried cranberries.

1 cup wheat berries, rinsed
1 bunch watercress, washed and dried, roughly chopped (about 2 cups)
1 large carrot, peeled and grated
1/2 cup dried cranberries, roughly chopped
Grated zest of 1 orange
Grated zest of 1 lime
1 cup pecans, toasted and chopped

CITRUS DRESSING
Juice of 1 orange (preferably blood orange)
Juice of 1 lime
1 tablespoon minced shallot
2 teaspoons maple syrup
3 tablespoons olive oil
1/2 teaspoon kosher salt

1 Add the wheat berries to a large saucepan filled with enough salted water to cover them by several inches. Bring to a boil, then reduce to a simmer, partially cover, and cook the wheat berries until they are plump and tender, about 75 to 90 minutes. Test as you cook; cooked wheat berries are still somewhat chewy. Drain and set aside to cool completely.

2 Add the watercress to the wheat berries, along with the carrot, cranberries and citrus zests.

3 To make the dressing, in a small bowl, whisk together all of the dressing ingredients. Just before serving, combine dressing with the wheat berries and gently mix. Garnish with toasted nuts. If you're not serving the salad the same day, store it and the dressing separately, covered, in the refrigerator.

SERVES 8 TO 10

CURRIED WHEAT BERRY SALAD WITH PISTACHIO NUTS AND COCONUT

This salad has a zingy curry-lime dressing and is topped with a sprinkling of shredded coconut and fiber-rich pistachio nuts.

1 cup wheat berries, rinsed

1/2 cup raisins, roughly chopped

3 celery stalks, cut in half lengthwise and thinly sliced

4 scallion greens, very thinly sliced

1/4 cup unsweetened, shredded dried coconut (optional)

1/2 cup whole shelled pistachio nuts or toasted sliced almonds

CURRY-LIME DRESSING

3 tablespoons fresh lime juice

2 teaspoons curry powder

1/2 teaspoon kosher salt

1/4 cup olive oil

1 Add the wheat berries to a large saucepan filled with enough salted water to cover them by several inches. Bring to a boil, then reduce to a simmer, partially cover, and cook the wheat berries until they are plump and tender, about 75 to 90 minutes. Test as you cook; cooked wheat berries are still somewhat chewy. Drain and set aside to cool completely.

2 In a large serving bowl, combine cooled wheat berries with the raisins, celery and scallions.

3 To make the dressing, in a small bowl, whisk together all of the dressing ingredients. Combine the dressing with the salad and garnish with shredded coconut if using, and pistachio nuts or sliced almonds.

VARIATIONS Add red pepper for color and sweetness, 1 teaspoon fresh minced ginger for a little more zing, and chickpeas, parsley or cilantro. Use different baby greens, watercress or mizuna, and try a variety of nuts for the garnish.

GREEK SALAD WITH FARRO

Farro is an ancient grain making a modern comeback. Like other grains, it has a nutty flavor and plenty of nutrients. Farro's shape and texture is similar to that of barley. In fact, you can substitute barley, wheat berries or spelt berries if farro is unavailable. Just follow the cooking times given for those grains in the chapter introduction. Whichever grain you use, this salad is deliciously chewy and quite refreshing with cucumbers, dill and mint. Do include the feta cheese for a salty contrast.

1 cup farro, rinsed
1 cucumber, peeled, seeded and diced
1 red bell pepper, cored and diced
1/4 cup minced red onion
1/4 cup minced fresh dill or parsley
1/4 cup chopped fresh mint
1 cup crumbled or diced feta cheese

RED WINE VINAIGRETTE
3 tablespoons red wine vinegar
1 clove garlic, finely minced
1/2 teaspoon kosher salt
1/4 cup olive oil

1 Place farro in a large saucepan and cover with 2 quarts of salted water. Bring to a boil, reduce heat and simmer, uncovered, about 30 to 35 minutes. Farro has a similar texture to barley when cooked. Drain well and set aside to cool completely.

2 In a large serving bowl, combine the farro, cucumber, red pepper, onion, dill or parsley and mint.

3 To make the dressing, in a small bowl, whisk together all of the dressing ingredients and combine well with the salad. Fold in the feta cheese. If there is any salad left over, bring it to room temperature and refresh it with a bit of lemon juice before serving.

VARIATIONS Include 1 cup of cooked chickpeas for added protein. Other ingredients to experiment with include black pitted olives, chopped tomatoes, capers and greens such as baby arugula, watercress or mizuna.

SERVES 10 TO 12

WILD RICE AND WHEAT BERRY SALAD WITH CRANBERRIES AND PINE NUTS

This is a perfect salad for a party. The combination of wild rice and wheat berries makes a hearty, but elegant fall or winter dish that's filled out with dried cranberries, diced apple and buttery pine nuts. If you can't find wheat berries, substitute 2 cups cooked brown or white rice.

3/4 cup wheat berries, rinsed
1 cup wild rice, rinsed
1 & 1/2 teaspoons kosher salt
2/3 cup dried cranberries, roughly chopped
1/2 cup thinly sliced celery
1 crisp apple, peeled and diced
1/2 cup minced parsley
1/4 cup pine nuts

CITRUS VINAIGRETTE

Grated zest of 1 lemon

1 tablespoon fresh lemon juice

Grated zest from 1 orange

1/2 cup fresh orange juice

2 tablespoons vinegar (balsamic, Champagne, raspberry or rice vinegar)

1 tablespoon finely minced shallot

2 teaspoons honey

1/4 cup olive oil

1/2 to 1 teaspoon kosher salt

1 In a large pot, bring at least 4 quarts of water and the wheat berries to a boil. Reduce heat to low and simmer, covered, for 35 minutes. Add the wild rice and salt to the pot. Bring to a boil again, lower the heat, then simmer and cook, partially covered, for an additional 50 to 55 minutes or until both grains are cooked. Many of the wild rice grains will have split somewhat, but they will still have a little bite. The wheat berries will be plump and slightly chewy. Drain well. Stir in the dried cranberries and let the mixture cool completely.

2 In a large serving bowl, combine the cooled grains and cranberries with the celery, apple and parsley. In a small bowl, whisk together all of the vinaigrette ingredients. Add the dressing to the salad and mix well; garnish with nuts. Serve at room temperature.

SERVES 6

JAN'S BARLEY-CORN SALAD

This salad came about when I was attending a potluck beach barbecue. During the party, a few people came up to ask me if I had made the delicious barley and corn salad they were enjoying. I hadn't, but after yet another guest had asked me, I decided to find out who had. It was no surprise when I learned that its creator was Jan Buhrman, a top caterer on Martha's Vineyard. Jan's recipe is a testament to the phrase "less is more." She makes this fabulous salad using fresh summer corn from Morning Glory Farm and often plays around with the ratio of corn to barley, depending on what's available in her catering kitchen.

6 ears fresh corn
1 cup cooked barley, page 189
Chopped chives, for garnish

LIME-CUMIN DRESSING
Grated zest of two limes
Juice of 4 limes
1 tablespoon ground cumin
2 tablespoons olive oil
Salt and pepper

1 Shuck corn and steam until just cooked, about 3 to 4 minutes. When cool enough to handle, cut the kernels off of the cob.

2 In a serving bowl, combine the steamed corn kernels and cooked barley.

3 Zest the limes directly into the bowl in which you will make the dressing, catching the tangy oils. Whisk together all of the dressing ingredients and pour the dressing over the corn and barley mixture. Toss well and garnish with chopped chives.

CORN OFF THE COB Fresh corn makes a colorful, sweet and crunchy addition to all kinds of salads. Removing the kernels from the cob is easy. Stand the ear on one end in a large bowl. Take a sharp knife and slice down the cob from top to bottom, right along the edge. The kernels fall neatly into the bowl.

TABOULI SALAD WITH TOMATOES, CUCUMBERS, PARSLEY AND MINT

Tabouli is a healthful, refreshing Mediterranean favorite made with bulgur wheat, parsley, mint, tomatoes, olive oil and lemon juice. Bulgur is one of the easiest grains to prepare—just pour boiling water over it and let it rest. You can make a completely balanced meal of this salad by adding cooked chickpeas or solid white tuna. It's also a terrific side dish with grilled kababs, fish, lamb dishes or spinach pie.

1 cup bulgur
2 pinches salt
2 tomatoes, seeded and diced
1 cucumber, peeled, seeded and diced
3 scallion greens, chopped
1 cup fresh parsley, finely minced
1/2 cup fresh mint leaves, chopped

LEMON DRESSING
3 tablespoons fresh lemon juice
3 tablespoons olive oil
1 clove garlic, minced
1/2 teaspoon kosher salt

1 Place the bulgur in a medium bowl, add 1 & 1/4 cups boiling water and the salt. Cover the bowl with a plate and let rest for about 20 minutes, or until the water is absorbed. Remove plate; let cool.

2 Fluff the bulgur with a fork. Add the tomato, cucumber, scallion, parsley and mint.

3 To make the dressing, in a small bowl, combine dressing ingredients and add to the salad just a few minutes before serving.

SERVES 6 TO 8

203
·
RAISING
THE
SALAD
BAR
·

QUINOA SALAD WITH LEMON VINAIGRETTE

This is one of my personal favorites. Friends often request this quinoa salad and I happily oblige because it's a snap to make and goes well with everything. The quinoa cooks in 15 minutes, and just a simple dressing of lemon juice and olive oil seasons it perfectly.

1 cup quinoa, rinsed
1/4 teaspoon kosher salt
1 bunch watercress, roughly chopped
(about 2 cups)
1 cucumber, peeled, seeded and diced
1 large carrot, peeled and grated
5 radishes, cut into matchsticks or grated
1 roasted red bell pepper, diced

LEMON VINAIGRETTE
1/4 cup fresh lemon juice
1/3 cup olive oil
1/2 teaspoon kosher salt

1 Add quinoa, salt and 1 & 1/2 cups water to a saucepan. Bring to a boil and then reduce heat to low, cover, and cook for 13 to 15 minutes, until the water is absorbed. Turn off the heat and let the quinoa sit for 5 minutes. Set aside to cool completely.

2 In a large serving bowl, combine the cooled quinoa, watercress, cucumber, carrot, radishes and red pepper.

3 To make the dressing, in a small bowl, whisk together all of the dressing ingredients. Add to the quinoa and vegetables and toss gently to combine. If there is any salad left over, refresh it with a bit of lemon juice and olive oil and serve at room temperature.

THE SUPER GRAIN Quinoa offers 20 different amino acids that your body uses to maintain and repair tissues, including all of the essential amino acids—making it a complete source of protein without the fat and calories found in meat. It is also a good source of iron, calcium, potassium and magnesium which helps to regulate blood pressure.

COOL SLAWS

COOL SLAWS

There's a special place on the American table for coleslaw. Crisp and cooling, it complements spicy barbecue dishes, smoky grilled meats, fish and burgers.

With a little creativity in the kitchen, slaws can be more than mere vehicles for mayonnaise. Cabbages—both red and green—have a clean, sweet taste that work in combination with fresh fennel, jicama, celery, red and yellow bell peppers and colorful radishes. Some slaws become really special with the addition of pineapple, either diced or cut into thin strips, orange sections, apples, grapes, mango or papaya. The Jicama, Mango and Green Cabbage Slaw on page 213—shredded cabbage with julienned mango and jicama splashed with citrus dressing—is a good example. Or try a red cabbage salad with bites of fresh pineapple and a pineapple-lime dressing.

There are many ways to let green and red cabbages shine, yet still save a place for the great classic coleslaws. Even they can be energized with wasabi, horseradish or chipotle peppers.

Asian cabbages offer even more possibilities. Chinese cabbages like Napa cabbage and bok choy are mild and sweet with a succulence that is perfect for slaws. They slice with ease and mix well with your favorite dressings.

Several other vegetables make creative slaws on their own, such as carrots, fennel, celery, celery root, radishes, and even beets. A salad of shredded carrots with greens is gorgeous to look at, and has a flavor that really surprises people.

There are also lots of nutritional benefits to slaws as well. Cabbages are members of the cruciferous family, like kale and broccoli, with a component called sulforaphane which helps stimulate enzymes that guard against the development of certain cancerous tumors. They also contain indoles that stimulate the body to break down estrogen into less potent forms and may help in reducing the incidence of breast cancer. Other key cabbage nutrients include vitamin C, beta carotene, fiber and folic acid, and the Chinese cabbages are particularly high in calcium.

There are several ways to go about prepping cabbage into long, thin strips for these recipes.

Slicing by Hand

These days, I use a mandoline for slicing cabbage, but for many years before that I did very well using a sharp, 8-inch chef's knife. Take a whole head of red or green cabbage and slice in half. Cut the half in two, straight down the middle. Hold each quarter of cabbage upright, stem end down, and cut out the core. Now it's ready for slicing. Because you want very thin strips or shreds, shave the sides of the cabbage for the thinnest pieces.

A medium head of cabbage yields between 8 to 10 cups of shredded cabbage.

Vegetable Slicers and Mandolines

I have to admit that I was a latecomer to using a vegetable slicer, or mandoline, because they seemed a bit complicated and dangerous—and I've never been a gadget type of person. But I'm happy to say that I've successfully crossed over to the other side. I bought the least expensive, simplest model— one of the plastic vegetables slicers found in Asian markets and kitchen supply stores—and found that it was extremely easy to use. Paper-thin strands of cabbage are produced in minutes. So slaw lovers shouldn't wait as long as I did to make this discovery.

There are many other types of vegetable slicers that can turn a head of cabbage into paper-thin slices with minimal effort. There are expensive professional-style French mandolines, plastic slicers from Japan, and quite a few others in between. If you're primarily interested in slicing cabbages and other vegetables, the inexpensive Japanese benriner versions are uncomplicated and do the job efficiently. Use these for thin slices of celery, fennel, onions, carrots, apples and other foods you like to shred as well.

To use the slicer, cut the whole head of cabbage head into quarters and remove the core. Set one quarter on the slicer, slanting away from you. Use gentle pressure to move the cabbage forward from the top to the bottom, and then up again to repeat. Keep pressure steady throughout to ensure even slices. Many kitchen stores offer demonstrations of several models. From these, you'll get a first-hand lesson in mastering these useful kitchen tools.

Food Processor

Food processors usually come with a shredding disk—it's the one with a lot of holes. Dig it out, if you haven't already. It's invaluable for making carrot, beet or fennel slaws. In seconds, it easily shreds a pound of carrots.

I don't usually use the food processor for cabbage slaws because I think the longer shreds that you get from slicing look prettier.

CABBAGES TO USE FOR SLAWS

Green

Smooth, round and compact, this cabbage is crisp when fresh and raw, and has a mild cabbage taste. Green cabbage keeps very well in the refrigerator.

Savoy

Savoy cabbage is less compact and its leaves are curled and more crumpled-looking than green cabbage. The flavor is sweeter and more delicate than that of green cabbage, making it a good choice for coleslaws and salads.

Red

Purple or reddish in color, red cabbage is not as sweet as green cabbage and its texture can be a bit tougher. But it has more vitamin C than green cabbage, providing the daily recommended amount in a single half-cup serving. Its color looks absolutely beautiful in slaws, either by itself or mixed with green cabbage, vegetables or fruits. Thinly shredded red cabbage also adds great color to leafy green salads.

Chinese Cabbage

There are two types of Chinese cabbage: one, often labeled as such, has a thin, elongated body with light green leaves. The other variety, Napa cabbage, is barrel-shaped, with pale green and white overlapping leaves that are crinkled and have a wide, ridged base. All parts of both varieties are edible. Thinly sliced, they make a crisp, juicy slaw that is usually dressed with Asian flavorings.

Bok choy

Bok choy has long, ivory-colored stalks and broad, dark green leaves. Crunchy and mild-tasting, it makes a perfect addition to Asian chicken or noodle salads. Its high water content also means that it sheds water quickly, so when used in coleslaw, it is best when dressed just before serving.

CLASSIC COLESLAW

This recipe recreates the classic taste of traditional coleslaw, but has a tangy dressing that's more like a vinaigrette, with some mayonnaise added for creaminess.

5 cups finely sliced green cabbage (about 1/2 head)

1 cup shredded carrots

3 tablespoons minced parsley or chopped chives

DRESSING

2 tablespoons apple cider vinegar

2 teaspoons sugar

1/3 cup mayonnaise

1/4 cup canola or grapeseed oil

Salt and pepper

5 or 6 drops of hot sauce

1 In a serving bowl, mix the cabbage, carrots and parsley or chives.

2 In a small bowl, whisk together the vinegar and sugar until the sugar dissolves. Whisk in the mayonnaise and oil; add salt, pepper and hot sauce to taste. Taste-test the dressing on a few spoonfuls of slaw, adjusting the salt and pepper if necessary. Just before serving, mix the dressing with the coleslaw.

VARIATIONS Substitute 1 tablespoon of fresh lemon juice for the vinegar. For some added color, replace some of the green cabbage with red cabbage.

SLAW WITH FRESH PINEAPPLE

Crunchy strands of cabbage and carrot with bites of fresh pineapple make this an attractive, cooling slaw.

4 or 5 cups thinly sliced red cabbage (about 1/2 head)

2 medium carrots, peeled and shredded

3 scallion greens, thinly sliced

2 cups fresh pineapple, cut into 1/2-inch dice

PINEAPPLE VINAIGRETTE

1/2 cup pineapple juice

2 tablespoons rice vinegar

1 tablespoon finely minced shallot

3 tablespoons canola or grapeseed oil

1/4 teaspoon kosher salt

1 In a large bowl, combine the cabbage, carrots and scallions.

2 In a small bowl, whisk together all of the dressing ingredients. Just before serving, generously dress the slaw and stir in the diced pineapple.

VARIATION For a spicy-sweet accent, add 2 or 3 teaspoons of Asian sweet chili sauce, the kind used as a dip for spring rolls.

SERVES 6

WASABI COLESLAW

Once it's mixed in a dressing, wasabi becomes considerably toned down, but still gives a delicious kick to coleslaw. It's best to make the dressing 10 to 15 minutes before serving to allow the wasabi's heat and flavor to fully develop.

6 cups thinly sliced green cabbage (about 1/2 head)

1 cup shredded carrots

3 tablespoons sliced scallion greens or minced parsley

WASABI DRESSING
5 teaspoons wasabi powder

2 tablespoons apple cider vinegar

2 teaspoons sugar

1/3 cup mayonnaise

1/4 cup canola or grapeseed oil

Several drops hot sauce

Salt and pepper

1 In a large bowl, combine the cabbage, carrots and scallions or parsley.

2 In a small bowl, add 2 & 1/2 teaspoons of water to the wasabi powder and mix until a paste forms. Set aside. In a separate bowl, whisk together the vinegar and sugar until the sugar dissolves. Whisk in the mayonnaise, oil and hot sauce; then add the wasabi paste, and salt and pepper. Mix well.

3 Just before serving, toss the dressing with the slaw.

WASABI POWDER Many brands of wasabi powder are actually blends of horseradish, mustard and green food coloring. Real wasabi, which is very flavorful, is often left out. If possible, find a brand that lists the real thing as an ingredient.

SERVES 6 TO 8

213
·
RAISING
THE
SALAD
BAR
·

JICAMA, MANGO AND GREEN CABBAGE SLAW WITH CITRUS VINAIGRETTE

This light, refreshing slaw is one of my favorites. It's a combination of shredded green cabbage with strips of fresh juicy mango and jicama, a sweet root vegetable shaped like a turnip, with crisp, juicy apple-like flesh. If you can't find jicama, substitute daikon radish, cut into matchsticks, red radishes or celery. This slaw is especially good with fish, among many other main-course dishes.

1 mango

1/4 pound jicama (about one quarter of a medium-sized jicama)

4 cups thinly sliced green cabbage (about 1/2 head)

1 red bell pepper, cored and thinly sliced

4 or 5 scallion greens, thinly sliced

CITRUS VINAIGRETTE

1/2 cup fresh orange juice

4 tablespoons fresh lime juice

2 teaspoons light vinegar, such as apple cider vinegar, rice vinegar or Champagne vinegar

2 teaspoons finely minced fresh ginger

2 teaspoons honey or sugar

3 tablespoons canola or grapeseed oil

Salt

1 Peel and cut the mango according to the directions on page 24. Once you have cut the flesh away from the pit, cut each slice into 1/8- to 1/4-inch thick strips.

2 Cut the jicama into 1/8-inch thick slices then cut each slice into 1/8-inch thick strips. You should have about 1 cup. In a large serving bowl, toss the jicama with the reserved mango, cabbage, bell pepper, and scallions.

3 In a small bowl, whisk together the citrus, vinegar, ginger, honey or sugar, and oil. Add salt to taste. Just before serving generously dress the slaw and mix well.

VARIATIONS Add 1/2 cup finely chopped cilantro in place of the scallions. For more striking color, add a cup of finely shredded red cabbage. Substitute mild Napa cabbage for the green cabbage, using the same amount.

SERVES 6

CARROT-FENNEL SLAW

This carrot and fennel slaw is a light, refreshing change from cabbage slaws and fits right in with barbecue, grilled foods, burgers of all kinds...just about anything. Use the food processor's shredding disk to quickly grate the fennel and carrot. Dry mustard adds a real kick to the dressing, but it takes time for the flavor to develop, so make the dressing first.

1 small to medium fennel bulb

3 cups peeled, shredded carrots (about 4 or 5 large carrots)

1/4 minced red onion

1/2 cup chopped fresh cilantro

1/3 cup toasted sliced almonds

DRESSING

5 tablespoons fresh orange juice

1 tablespoon Champagne vinegar (or other light vinegar)

2 teaspoons fresh lemon juice

1 to 1 & 1/2 teaspoons dry mustard

2 tablespoons olive oil

1/2 teaspoon kosher salt

1 In a small bowl, whisk together all of the dressing ingredients.

2 Remove the top greens and stalks from the fennel bulb, saving the feathery fennel greens for the slaw. Use a vegetable peeler to remove any bruised or tough spots. Quarter the trimmed bulb and cut out the core. Shred half of the fennel (reserve other half for another use) using the shredding disk of your food processor, or grate it by hand. You should have about 1 cup. In a medium bowl, combine the fennel with the carrots, red onion and cilantro.

3 Just before serving, pour dressing over slaw and mix well. Garnish with toasted almonds.

SHREDDED BEET SLAW WITH MICRO-GREENS

Shredding the beets for this pretty slaw cuts their cooking time to just 4 minutes! Sweet orange sections top off the earthy beets, and combined with spicy micro-greens and some tangy goat cheese, this is the perfect salad course for a dinner party. Both the dressing and the beets can be prepared ahead.

2 medium to large beets, peeled

2 cups micro-arugula, mâche, watercress or other baby greens

Sections from 2 oranges

1/4 cup walnuts, toasted and chopped

4 ounces goat cheese, crumbled

ORANGE-MUSTARD VINAIGRETTE

4 tablespoons fresh orange juice

1/2 teaspoon Dijon mustard

1 tablespoon Champagne vinegar, apple cider vinegar or rice vinegar

2 teaspoons finely minced shallot

2 tablespoons olive oil

Pinch of salt

1 Shred beets using the shredding disk on your food processor, or grate with a hand grater. Steam the shredded beets for 4 minutes, then spread them out on a large plate or sheet tray and let cool.

2 In a bowl, whisk together all of the dressing ingredients.

3 Place the beets and micro-greens in separate bowls. Just before serving, generously dress each bowl of ingredients, mixing well. Reserve any leftover dressing for another salad or slaw. Divide micro-greens among 4 plates. Top each serving with some of the shredded beets, then arrange 2 or 3 orange sections on top of the beets. Top with toasted walnuts and goat cheese.

SERVES 6 TO 8

RED CABBAGE SLAW WITH LEMON-GINGER VINAIGRETTE

Striking colors, fantastic flavors and satisfying crunch all in one fabulous slaw! This personal favorite is a refreshing change in the winter. Serve it on the side any time of year to kick up burgers, steak or fish.

4 cups thinly sliced red cabbage (about 1/2 head)

1 red bell pepper, cored and cut into very thin strips

1 large carrot, peeled and shredded or cut into matchsticks

1 cup snow peas, strings removed

2 tablespoons toasted sesame seeds

LEMON-GINGER VINAIGRETTE

1 tablespoon raspberry vinegar or rice vinegar

2 tablespoons fresh lemon juice

1 tablespoon soy sauce

1 teaspoon finely-minced fresh ginger

4 teaspoons maple syrup or honey

3 tablespoons canola oil

1 tablespoon toasted sesame oil

1 In a serving bowl, combine the shredded red cabbage, red bell pepper and carrots. Blanch snow peas in boiling water for 1 minute and then run them under cold water to stop the cooking. Slice each snow pea lengthwise into 3 thin strips and add to the bowl.

2 In a small bowl, whisk together all of the dressing ingredients. Mix a bit of dressing with a spoonful or two of slaw. Taste-test the flavors—the dressing should be pleasantly balanced between sweet and sour; if it isn't, adjust ingredients accordingly. Just before serving, dress the slaw and garnish with toasted sesame seeds.

VARIATIONS Add protein to the slaw and turn it into a main-course meal by mixing in 1 or 2 cups cooked, shredded chicken. For a striking presentation, use black sesame seeds as a garnish, or try chopped, unsalted roasted peanuts instead of sesame seeds. You can also add a cup of broccoli florets, steamed for 3 minutes and cooled under cold running water.

GARDEN VEGGIE SALADS

GARDEN VEGGIE SALADS

The abundance of summer vegetables is irresistible, which makes it easy to go overboard and buy too much of too many. These salads can help use up your surplus in good-for-you, great-tasting ways.

Most of these vegetable salads are quite easy to assemble, and they're perfect in the summer when cooking is best kept to a minimum. Good examples are Laura Silber's Fresh Corn Salad, which uses fresh, uncooked summer corn with bits of tomato, avocado, lime and cilantro, or the refreshing, simple combination of cucumber and watercress with Thai dressing. The cucumber-yogurt salad is another refreshing combination that can do triple duty as a side dish, sauce or as an appetizer served with pita bread.

Single vegetable salads work nicely alongside leafy green, pasta or potato salads and grilled or barbecued foods. A salad of thin haricots verts tastes just like springtime when served at room temperature, and the elegant beans can be garnished with goat cheese or blue cheese and a sprinkling of pine nuts or chopped walnuts. Their cooking time is only about 4 minutes, so preparation is very quick, especially if a helper trims the beans.

The trick to getting the recipes in this chapter just right is to cook the vegetables properly.

Green Beans

Slender, delicate green beans make simple, appealing salads—especially if they keep their bright green color, and are cooked just right: with just a tiny bit of crunch. Steaming them is a quick and easy method that yields good results. While you bring a pot of water to a boil, rinse the beans and trim the stems. If you like to trim both ends, you can cut them on the diagonal for a neat presentation. While bean sizes vary, I've had the best luck steaming green beans and haricots verts for 4 or 5 minutes. At 4 minutes, taste a green bean to gauge its degree of doneness. Then test every 30 seconds until the beans are cooked. They should be tender but still slightly crisp. Immediately remove the beans from heat and run them under cold water until they're cool to the touch. (You can also plunge the beans, as well as the other vegetables in this chapter, into a bowl filled with ice water to stop the cooking.)

Cauliflower

Cut cauliflower into uniform, bite-size florets and steam for 4 to 6 minutes, until they're tender but not too soft or falling apart. You should be able to pierce a floret with a fork, but still feel some resistance. Begin testing at 4 min-utes and then at 30 second intervals until cauliflower is done. Immediately run under cold water until cool to the touch. Drain excess water on paper towels.

Broccoli

Cut broccoli into uniform-size florets and steam for 3 minutes. You should be able to pierce a floret with a fork, but still feel some resistance. Broccoli should be tender, but not too soft. Immediately run under cold water to stop the cooking. Drain any excess water on paper towels.

Snow peas

Snow peas keep their color best when they're just blanched in boiling water. While you bring the water to a boil, remove the strings from the snow peas. Add them to the water and boil for 30 seconds, or just until they're bright green. Drain and run under cold water. Drain excess water on paper towels.

Corn off the Cob

When making a corn salad, corn shaved right off the cob tastes best. Its slight crunch and sweet taste add so much to a salad. You can cook the corn off the cob or on the cob, but I think it's easiest to remove the kernels first and then cook them.

Slice the kernels from the cob as described on page 24. Steam the kernels for 3 to 5 minutes or boil for just a minute or two. I've never cooked corn for more than a couple of minutes, but when chef Laura Silber stirred raw corn kernels into her avocado and tomato salad, it was a revelation that fresh, raw corn could taste so good.

Asparagus

The traditional method for cooking asparagus—in a pot of simmering water—works well, but the asparagus tend to get slightly waterlogged. I find that sautéing the asparagus in a pan is a much better technique.

Start with a pound of asparagus and trim off the bottom 2 inches of each stalk. Diagonally cut the stalks into 1- to 1 & 1/2-inch pieces. Preheat a large, heavy skillet or cast iron pan until it's hot and add 1 tablespoon olive oil or enough to lightly coat the pan and the asparagus pieces. Cook until just crisp-tender, about 4 minutes, stirring frequently. Remove pan from heat and let cool. The asparagus will continue to cook as it cools, but not enough to detract from its crispness.

To cook asparagus in water, bring 1 inch of water to a boil in a medium sauté pan. Add the asparagus pieces in a single layer and cook, covered, until tender but still crisp, about 2 or 3 minutes. Drain the asparagus and run under cold water to stop the cooking; drain again. Drain any excess water from the asparagus on paper towels.

CHICKPEA AND CAULIFLOWER SALAD WITH LEMON-JALAPEÑO DRESSING

Cauliflower and chickpeas make a surprisingly good combination, especially with the addition of fresh tomatoes, red onion and cilantro. Be careful not to overcook (or undercook) the cauliflower. Because tomatoes don't hold up too well or taste their best once they're refrigerated, this salad tastes best on the day it's made.

1 small to medium head of cauliflower, cut into florets (about 5 cups)
2 cups cherry tomatoes, quartered
1/4 red onion, sliced paper thin
1 cup canned chickpeas, rinsed and drained
1/2 cup chopped fresh cilantro

LEMON-JALAPEÑO DRESSING
4 tablespoons fresh lemon juice
1 jalapeño pepper, seeded and finely diced
1/4 cup olive oil
Salt and pepper

1 Cut the cauliflower into bite-size florets and steam for 4 to 6 minutes, until tender. You should be able to pierce the florets with a fork, but still have some resistance. Run the cauliflower under cold water until cool. Cut the florets into smaller pieces so they more closely match the size of the chickpeas. In a serving bowl, combine the cauliflower, tomatoes, red onion and chickpeas.

2 In a small bowl, whisk together all of the dressing ingredients.

3 Just before serving, combine the dressing with the salad. Stir in the chopped cilantro and mix well.

SERVES 6

FRESH CORN SALAD

Creamy bites of avocado, crunchy fresh raw corn and a touch of cilantro and lime make this a summer salad sent straight from heaven. Actually, it comes from friend Laura Silber, a private chef on Martha's Vineyard, who never seems to take a wrong step when it comes to cooking. She adds raw corn kernels to all kinds of salads. This recipe couldn't be easier.

Kernels from 6 ears of fresh corn
1 tomato, seeded and diced
1 firm but ripe avocado, diced
2 scallions, thinly sliced or 2 tablespoons finely chopped red onion
1/4 cup chopped fresh cilantro

LIME DRESSING
2 tablespoons fresh lime juice
1/2 teaspoon finely minced garlic
3 tablespoons olive oil
Salt and pepper

1 In a large serving bowl, remove corn kernels as described on page 24. Combine with the tomato, avocado and scallions.

2 To make the dressing, in a small bowl, whisk together all of the dressing ingredients. Combine the dressing with the salad and gently mix. Garnish with chopped cilantro.

SERVES 6 TO 8

227
·
RAISING
THE
SALAD
BAR
·

HEIRLOOM TOMATO, FRESH MOZZARELLA AND BREAD SALAD

The combination of tomatoes, fresh mozzarella, torn basil and bread makes a wonderful salad during tomato season. I'd suggest preparing the tomatoes close to the time the salad will be served because they will lose flavor if refrigerated.

2 pounds mixed heirloom tomatoes (include green, yellow and red, plus some cherry tomatoes)

1/2 loaf French or Italian bread, cut into cubes (3 to 4 cups)

1 tablespoon olive oil

Salt and pepper

10 to 12 ounces fresh mozzarella cheese, cut into bite-size pieces

1/3 cup toasted pine nuts

1 cup fresh basil leaves, torn

RED WINE VINAIGRETTE

3 tablespoons red wine vinegar

1 tablespoon finely minced shallot

1 teaspoon finely minced garlic

1/2 cup olive oil

Salt and pepper

1 Cut the tomatoes in various ways—small wedges, a few thick, quartered slices, and whole and halved cherry tomatoes. Place in a bowl and set aside.

2 Preheat oven to 375°. Place cubed bread on a baking sheet and drizzle with the oil and season with salt and pepper. Bake the bread until lightly golden, about 12 to 15 minutes. Set aside.

3 To make the dressing, in a small bowl, combine the vinegar, shallot and garlic, then whisk in the oil. Season with salt and pepper.

4 Just before serving, drain the tomatoes of excess liquid and mix in the mozzarella. Pour the vinaigrette over both. Add the bread and mix gently. Top with the pine nuts and torn basil.

THE BEST FRESH MOZZARELLA Maplebrook Farm, a cheese-making business in Vermont, makes the most delectable, creamy and slightly salted fresh mozzarella. Michael Scheps, a third-generation Sicilian-American cheese maker, makes his mozzarella by hand the way his father and grandfather did, presiding over each step. And it shows. Try it in pasta salads, too. Maplebrook mozzarella can be found at Whole Foods Markets around New England. For other good fresh mozzarella, check out Italian markets or local artisans.

GREEN BEAN AND RADICCHIO SALAD

Crisp green beans team up with slightly bitter but beautiful radicchio. Toasty nuts and goat cheese nicely balance the flavors and textures.

1 pound fresh green beans (use haricots verts if available), ends trimmed
1 cup thinly sliced radicchio
1/3 cup walnuts, toasted and chopped
4 ounces goat cheese, crumbled

LEMON DRESSING
1 tablespoon fresh lemon juice
1 small clove garlic, finely minced
3 tablespoons olive oil
Salt and pepper

1 Steam green beans until crisp tender, approximately 4 to 5 minutes. Immediately run the green beans under cold water until cool. Drain well and pat dry with paper towels. Soak the radicchio in a salad spinner filled with cold water for 10 minutes to remove some of its bitterness. Lift the spinner insert, drain the water, and spin the radicchio dry. Place the beans and radicchio in a serving bowl.

2 To make the dressing, in a small bowl, whisk together all of the dressing ingredients. Just before serving, dress the salad and top with in the toasted walnuts and goat cheese.

SERVES 4

CUCUMBER AND WATERCRESS SALAD WITH THAI LIME DRESSING

I like the simplicity of fresh watercress with cucumbers, but this salad can easily adapt to a different leafy green and/or the addition of other vegetables.

1 bunch watercress, washed and dried, about 2 cups
2 medium cucumbers, peeled and seeded
1/3 cup roasted unsalted peanuts, chopped

THAI LIME DRESSING
2 & 1/2 tablespoons fresh lime juice
5 tablespoons canola oil
2 teaspoons sweet chili sauce
1/2 teaspoon finely minced garlic
1 teaspoon brown sugar
3 tablespoons chopped fresh mint (optional)
Pinch of salt

1 Remove any large stems from the watercress, leaving the smaller stems intact. Roughly chop. Cut the cucumbers into thin slices and combine with watercress in a serving bowl.

2 Place all of the dressing ingredients in a blender and process until mixture is creamy.

3 When ready to serve, generously dress the salad, and garnish with chopped peanuts.

MAKES ABOUT 2 & 1/2 CUPS

CUCUMBER-YOGURT SALAD

This is one of the most cooling, delicious combinations ever put together. Whenever I make it, I can't stop eating it. Serve it as a side dish, as a sauce with fish, grilled steak or lamb kababs, or as a dip with pita bread.

2 cups plain yogurt (Greek style or whole milk)
1 cucumber, peeled, seeded and diced
1 tablespoon olive oil
1/2 teaspoon ground cumin
1 teaspoon finely minced garlic
2 teaspoons fresh lemon juice
1/4 cup chopped fresh cilantro or mint
Salt and pepper
Pita bread for dipping

1 Drain the yogurt in a colander lined with a coffee filter or a few paper towels for about 20 to 30 minutes. It will become quite thick.

2 In a serving bowl, combine the yogurt, cucumber, oil, cumin, garlic, lemon juice, cilantro or mint, and salt and pepper.

3 Serve with pita bread cut into wedges for dipping.

SERVES 4 TO 6

231
·
RAISING
THE
SALAD
BAR
·

TOMATO AND CUCUMBER SALAD WITH HERBED VINAIGRETTE

This salad is simple and lovely. Serve it with grilled slices of crusty bread rubbed with a clove of garlic. If you haven't tried a French sheep's milk feta, such as valbresso, I suggest doing so—the flavor is wonderfully complex. You will probably have some leftover dressing; save it to drizzle over a green salad, green beans or grilled asparagus.

4 or 5 tomatoes, cored

1 cucumber, peeled, cut in half lengthwise and seeded

1/2 cup pitted kalamata olives, quartered lengthwise

Salt

1/2 cup feta cheese or blue cheese, crumbled

Basil leaves, for garnish

HERBED VINAIGRETTE

3 tablespoons sherry, balsamic, or red wine vinegar

1/2 cup olive oil

1 tablespoon each finely-chopped fresh oregano, basil and chives

Salt and pepper

1 Cut each tomato in half. Cut each half into bite-size wedges (at least four wedges per half). Thinly slice the cucumber.

2 Combine tomatoes, cucumber and olives in a large serving bowl or on a platter. Sprinkle with salt and toss gently to combine.

3 To make the dressing, in a small bowl, whisk together the vinegar and oil; mix in the herbs and season with salt and pepper. Just before serving, drizzle the desired amount of vinaigrette over the salad; scatter the feta or blue cheese over the top, but don't mix it in. At the last minute, tear the basil leaves and scatter the pieces over all.

DRESSING UP

DRESSING UP

If you're used to opening bottles of supermarket dressings for your salads, you'll be surprised by the freshness and flavor of ones you make yourself, and the vibrancy they give to salads. Most bottled dressings contain preservatives, additives, natural "flavors" and a long list of thickeners, stabilizers and other ingredients. They rarely contain the most healthful of oils, extra-virgin olive oil; instead, they are made with soybean oil, canola oil and other vegetable oils. Many have names that sound delicious, like Roasted Garlic and Rosemary, but whenever I've been tempted to try one, I am ultimately disappointed. This story illustrates my point:

At a relative's house not long ago, I was offered a salad of lettuce and vegetables that was nicely assembled from ingredients that had been bought that day. Accompanying it was a bottle of raspberry vinaigrette, which looked perfectly fine and evoked the anticipation of fresh-tasting raspberries atop fresh greens.

My first bite, however, extinguished my excitement. The dressing tasted strange, and it dominated the salad with an off-flavor, all too typical of the bottled dressings I've tried. What this salad needed was a freshly made vinaigrette. As those who make their own dressings know, once you're used to the homemade version, it's hard to enjoy anything else.

Making dressings from scratch is not complicated, nor is it time-consuming. And the payoff is well worth the few minutes you spend to make it.

This chapter gives you some simple guidelines, such as the basic ratio of oil to vinegar, flavor "extras" to enhance dressings, basic tools and a look at the variety of oils and vinegars that are available in today's markets.

Take a few minutes to familiarize yourself with these basics, then think about the process and try making a few dressings of your own. Once you've gone that far, it quickly becomes second nature. You'll be confident that whichever wonderful fresh ingredients you choose to combine, your dressing will make it all come together beautifully.

VINAIGRETTE BASICS

236
·
RAISING
THE
SALAD
BAR
·

The result you're looking for is a vinaigrette that's pleasing to taste—even delicious—not the tart, acidic vinaigrettes that usually come to mind.

A vinaigrette is a combination of two prime ingredients: oil and vinegar. The standard ratio is 3 tablespoons olive oil to 1 tablespoon vinegar. Depending on your own tastes and the type of vinegar you use, you are likely to veer from the standard ratio. With a mellow, aged balsamic vinegar, you may combine 1 tablespoon vinegar with just 2 tablespoons olive oil. For a sharper vinegar, like a sherry vinegar, the ratio might be more like 1 tablespoon vinegar to 4 or 5 tablespoons oil.

The role of citrus can play a big part in vinaigrettes. Freshly squeezed lime or lemon juice can be substituted completely for vinegar, and mixed with olive oil in approximately the same ratios. It's as easy as substituting 1 tablespoon lime or lemon juice for 1 tablespoon of the vinegar, and it can give the entire dressing a very fresh, bright flavor.

To make a simple vinaigrette, place the vinegar in a bowl and add oil in a thin, steady stream, whisking constantly to create a smooth, creamy dressing. Season with two or three pinches of salt and a few grinds of pepper. Dip a piece of lettuce into the vinaigrette to taste, and make any necessary adjustments that will create a balanced whole.

In general, 5 to 6 tablespoons of vinaigrette are enough for 4 to 6 servings, or about 10 to 12 cups of greens. To make an impromptu vinaigrette for a typical salad, my usual starting point is 2 tablespoons vinegar to 5 tablespoons oil.

Using a Blender, Food Processor or Mixing By Hand

You have more control of a vinaigrette when you mix it by hand. The oil can be added in a thin stream, whisking as it's added until the dressing is emulsified—that is, the oil and vinegar are thoroughly combined, without a trace of separation. The best tools for this job are small- to medium-size whisks and small- to medium-size metal bowls. Typically, after a mix of oil and vinegar sits out for a while, the two liquids will separate. This is fine; just remember to

briefly whisk again just before dressing the salad.

Certain ingredients can serve as emulsifiers in a dressing, keeping it thoroughly combined. These include mustard, eggs and mayonnaise.

From time to time, a blender does a good job of emulsifying, especially when no other emulsifier is used. You can add a whole garlic clove or piece of shallot, parsley or basil leaves, along with the oil and vinegar, and the blender will do the work of mincing and mixing.

A food processor serves a similar purpose and works best when liquid is minimal, such as in a homemade mayonnaise or pesto. I particularly like the food processor for Caesar salad dressings with anchovy fillets, garlic and lemon juice.

Tasting the Dressing

When you whisk a combination of ingredients, you can be your own judge and make any adjustments before tossing the vinaigrette with the salad. The best way to do this is by dipping a piece of lettuce into the dressing and taking a bite. What you initially taste on one leaf will be slightly stronger when it's mixed into the entire salad. If there's too much vinegar, add more oil. If it tastes bland, add a little more vinegar or salt.

A VERY QUICK DRESSING

When you're really in a rush, you can still make a perfect-tasting dressing by directly adding oil and vinegar to the salad. This technique starts with washed and dried salad greens placed in a serving bowl. Drizzle just enough olive oil over the greens to coat them, and gently mix with tongs, lifting from the bottom, until the oil is evenly distributed. Add a sprinkling of salt, then shake a few drops of vinegar over the salad. Mix and taste, adding additional drops of vinegar until the dressing is well-balanced. I usually reserve this method for the finest, most tasty vinegars on hand.

VINEGARS

238
·
RAISING
THE
SALAD
BAR
·

If you haven't yet experimented with some of the new vinegars on the market, it could make one of the biggest differences in your salads.

There has been a significant growth in the number vinegar producers, especially small producers using 100 percent aged red and white wines, as well as sparkling wines, to make a variety of vinegars with unique flavors. These are worlds away from highly diluted mass-produced supermarket vinegars, usually a blend of wine vinegar with harsh distilled white vinegar. To get acquainted with these vinegars, I'd suggest sampling and experimenting with one bottle from each of the categories described below.

Red Wine Vinegars

The term vinegar comes from the French words *vin aigre*, which translate as "sour wine." A few centuries ago, the port of Orleans in France was the center of the wine trade. Some wine would turn before it reached the city, but rather than waste it, inventive buyers used it in cooking. From those beginnings came the "Orleans" method of making vinegar: red wine is put into barrels with small openings that allow air to circulate while introducing a variety of bacterial cultures (acetobacters) that slowly turn the wine into vinegar, yet allow the wine to retain its essential character.

This is the key, say today's vinegar producers—retaining the essential character of the wine as it becomes vinegar. For salads, this means that each red wine vinegar has its own personality, flavor and fully partners with olive oil in dressing up a salad.

Here in the U.S., California's wine country has become the center of a vinegar renaissance, represented by artisan vinegar producers like Philip and Denise Toomey of Sparrow Lanes Vineyards.

The Toomeys, who consider wine as more of a food, had the idea of creating a line of vinegars based on different wines in the region. They began producing Zinfandel vinegar, Merlot vinegar, even a golden balsamic from Chardonnay, as their line grew.

The wine for their vinegars comes from local wine producers who may have an overrun of wine where the ph is slightly off the ideal for drinking. "The beauty of this wine is many of them come aged," Toomey explains.

They take the wine, and convert it to acetic acid using bacterial cultures or enzymes. During the process, pumps are used to oxidate the wine in stainless steel tanks. This conversion process takes several months. The couple treats making vinegar with as much care as winemakers do with their wines, looking at every part of the process with an eye toward improving the outcome. "We want to do it better," they say.

Interest in more flavorful vinegars has led to experimentation among producers. After barrel-aging their Zinfandel vinegar, the O Olive Oil Company of San Rafael, California, adds real bing cherry juice during the last two months of the process. "It tends to round it out a bit, taking a bit of edge out," said O Company Vice President Mario Aranda. Their sherry vinegar is combined with apricot wine in the final stages of aging to mellow the typical sharpness found in a sherry vinegar. Their best seller is a Champagne vinegar with a touch of citrus for brightness. Their Merlot comes straight out of the barrel unadorned, as does a new variety of a Port wine vinegar called PortO.

Aranda, who says the company is made up of "foodies" like himself, explains how different vinegars lend themselves to an infinite variety of salads and parings with greens. "Once you begin to pair vinegar with a particular kind of lettuce, you hit home runs often and never serve the same salad twice."

Baby lettuces, he says, love a crisp champagne vinegar. And he likes

VINEGARS

240
·
RAISING
THE
SALAD
BAR
·

Zinfandel vinegar with red leaf lettuce and a good Parmesan. "So simple. A little good salt and you're in heaven."

These two producers are among a number of others in California. There are also French and Italian vinegar makers with similar authentic wine vinegars.

Each time you need to buy a bottle of red wine vinegar, I'd suggest trying a sampling of new ones and picking out your favorites. Many of the vinegars range from $5 to $12 a bottle, and sometimes more. A Cabernet vinegar produced by St. Helena Oil Company of Napa Valley, barrel-aged for 19 years, sells for about $35.

Balsamic Vinegar

Most people today keep a bottle of balsamic vinegar handy, especially because it enhances so many types of salads. A rich, sweet-tart vinegar, balsamic is made from wine cooked down into a grape must and then aged. Typically, the longer it's aged, the more complex and mellow this vinegar becomes. Besides those basics, there are many brands, aged anywhere up to 25 years and longer, and a wide range of prices. When you're due for a new bottle, here again, it's good to try another brand to see if you like it any better than your last.

Cook's Illustrated did a taste test of supermarket balsamic vinegars under $10 and its panel recommended the Whole Foods 365 brand as the top, an import from Italy made with grape must.

When I tried it, it did taste better than the other moderately priced balsamics I had previously used. For balsamics that may not be as rich, complex and smooth as a multi-year aged one, I recommend adding a tiny bit of maple syrup to the vinaigrette. It adds just the right amount of sweetness, reminiscent of a more expensive bottle.

White Balsamic Vinegar

White balsamic is similar to a regular balsamic but made from white grapes, and like the others, has elements of sweetness in it. The benefit of a white balsamic is the clear color which won't "stain" ingredients. It also doesn't seem to wilt tender baby greens as readily as the traditional balsamic vinegar does.

Sparrow Lane Vineyards in California makes a really excellent white balsamic from a California Chardonnay.

White Wine, Champagne and Sherry Vinegars

This light-colored vinegar makes a good alternative to red wine vinegars for leafy green, potato, or pasta salads. Champagne vinegar is especially good combined with citrus such as fresh lemon, lime or orange juice.

In the course of my vinegar exploration, I mail-ordered a champagne vinegar from the St. Helena Olive Oil Company. The vinegar was the best I've ever tried, you could almost drink it. At $19 a bottle, however, I use it judiciously, and look forward to the flavor on each new salad.

St. Helena owner Peggy O'Kelly confirms that the quality of vinegar starts with the quality of wine. To make their champagne vinegar, her company uses a 10-year-old Napa Valley sparkling wine. Most producers don't make vinegar from actual champagne or sparkling wine, she says.

Sherry vinegar comes from Spain, home of sherry, and has a nutty, light flavor different from most red wine or white wine vinegars. It tends to be sharp and often needs a higher ratio of olive oil to vinegar than most vinaigrettes.

Fruit Vinegars

Fruit vinegars such as apple cider, raspberry, strawberry and fig vinegar, among others, are vinegars to which fruit is added, or in the case of apple cider vinegar, made entirely from apples. Fruit vinegars taste great with spicy baby green mixes or peppery greens like watercress or arugula, as well as green salads served with fruit on top, such as pears, apples, raspberries and blackberries. Apple cider vinegar, especially a quality one, makes a multi-purpose dressing that lets the taste of good greens shine though.

The key to finding a good fruit vinegar is reading the label for the addition of actual fruit. Most times, producers add fruit flavorings—so-called "natural flavors"—without any real fruit. These vinegars often have an off-flavor that comes across in the dressing, and the salad itself.

The gold standard for me is a raspberry vinegar made by Cheshire Gardens, located in New Hampshire. Owner Patti Powers calls this raspberry vinegar the "The Queen of Hearts." A second-generation raspberry farmer who began producing vinegars in the late '80s, Powers currently tends 700 feet of raspberries, grown without any chemicals or pesticides. During the season, she picks ripened raspberries every day, choosing the deep, dark red Heritage variety for her vinegar. The picked raspberries are processed immediately, first pureed, then added in equal parts to a wine vinegar. The combo sits for several weeks before being double-filtered and heated gently with wildflower honey.

Timothy Smith's Shelburne Apple Company produces an apple cider vinegar that is made solely from pesticide-free apples and doesn't have the harsh acidic undertones typically found in supermarket varieties.

"There aren't too many places that make cider vinegar from actual apple cider," says Smith, who has been farming since 1980 on a farm that's been in existence since 1828. Smith says he grows a variety of apples that all go into the mix, including Macintosh and Cortland's. A neighboring farm presses the apples to make apple cider, and then a nearby farm converts the cider into hard cider. The final conversion into vinegar is done back at Shelburne Apple Co. and takes up to 4 months.

We're lucky to have such dedicated artisans, making quality products with so much flavor. We can do our part to continue their existence by purchasing these delicious natural vinegars.

If you can't find real fruit vinegars, try blending fresh fruit into a regular vinaigrette. A handful of ripe, sweet spring strawberries or raspberries adds a touch of color and delicious fruitiness. This can be done with pineapple, mango, peaches, cherries, figs—you get the idea.

Rice Vinegar

While most vinegars are in the range of 5 or 6 percent acidity, rice vinegar comes in at 4 percent, which makes it a more mellow vinegar, less tart than say a traditional red or white wine vinegar. Though it can be used for any vinaigrette, it's typically used in Asian-based salads. It complements ingredients such as soy sauce, sesame oil and miso.

Rice vinegar comes "seasoned" or "unseasoned." The seasoned variety has added salt and sugar. It's best to buy the unseasoned, so you can season to your own liking.

Some recommendations

Though based solely on my own personal opinion, I've made a list of some of my current favorite vinegars. It's not exhaustive and I'm sure there are many more great vinegars out there that I haven't tried. I look forward to continuing my exploration, and would be happy to hear from anyone with their own recommendations. Further sources are listed on page 262.

- **Cabernet Red Wine Vinegar, O Olive Oil Company (California)**
- **Zinfandel Red Wine Vinegar, O Olive Oil Company (California)**
- **White Balsamic Vinegar, Sparrow Lane Co. (California)**
- **Apple Cider Vinegar, Shelburne Apple Co. (Massachusetts)**
- **Champagne Vinegar, St. Helena Olive Oil Co. (California)**
- **Moscatel Vinegar, Unio Company (Spain)**
- **Queen of Hearts Raspberry Vinegar, Cheshire Garden (New Hampshire)**
- **Whole Foods 365 Balsamic Vinegar of Modena, Whole Foods Market (Texas-based food chain)**
- **Villa Manodori Aceto Balsamico di Modena (Italy), Available at Whole Foods**

OILS

Olive Oil

Much has been written about olive oil, in terms of both its health properties and various characteristics that depend on where the oil is produced. The three largest olive oil producing countries are Spain, Italy and Greece, respectively, producing 95 percent of the world's olive oil. Other countries that produce olive oil include the U.S., specifically California, where some excellent olive oils are currently being made.

The flavors of olive oil can range from mild, smooth and buttery to stronger olive flavors. A peppery taste in olive oil can cause a burning sensation in the back of the throat. The flavor profiles of different olive oils have been described as fruity, grassy, peppery, sweet, bland, and nutty, among others. The only way to determine your own preference is to sample some olive oils and find your favorite. Search for a good, all-purpose, extra-virgin, first cold pressing olive oil that is fruity or smooth (or mild as opposed to bold), with as little aftertaste as possible, to use on all of your salads.

Whichever brand you choose, always select an extra-virgin olive oil, considered the premium olive oil for its flavor, color and aroma. Extra-virgin is the first pressing of the olives, extracted without heat or chemicals; in essence, without any refinement. That's why it is also considered the most healthful olive oil.

Olive oil labeled "pure" is typically a blend of extra-virgin oil and refined olive oil. Extra-light and light olive oils are terms that refer to their color and aroma, not their fat content, and generally contain about 95 percent refined oil and 5 percent extra-virgin oil. These pale olive oils won't add much flavor to your salads.

Spain and Italy further grade their olive oils according to their percent of acidity, a means of measuring the maturity of olives when they were harvested. To be labeled extra-virgin, olive oil must have an acidity level of less than 1 percent. Olive oils labeled superfine virgin, fine-virgin, and virgin have higher levels—generally from 1 to 3 percent—which are often felt as a sharpness at the back of the throat.

The best place to store olive oil is in a cool, dark place. Do not store it in the refrigerator, however, as cold tends to cause condensation in the oil.

Canola or Grapeseed Oil

Canola oil is a neutral-flavored oil that's used like a vegetable oil. In this book, it's used in Asian dressings when you don't want a pronounced olive oil taste.

Grapeseed oil is also a good alternative to olive oil when seeking a neutral flavor. Grapeseed oil can enhance the flavors of ingredients instead of overpowering them, and it has no aftertaste. Another feature worth mentioning—it

has some emulsification properties that make it useful in preparing dressings that will not separate when chilled.

Grapeseed oil is high in vitamin E and contains omega-6 oil, an essential fatty acid.

Sesame Oil

Toasted sesame oil offers dressings a characteristically Asian, nut-like flavor. A few teaspoons are all that are usually needed, a little goes a long way.

Sesame oil tends to turn rancid quickly. If you keep the bottle in the refrigerator, it will last longer.

Nut Oils

If they're from a top-quality producer, nut oils such as walnut and hazelnut impart a rich, toasted taste to vinaigrettes. They're especially tasty when used in place of extra-virgin olive oil, or combined with it, to dress mixed baby greens, arugula and salads with roasted pears and specialty cheeses. Walnut oil is rich in healthful fatty acids.

My dilemma regarding nut oils is that I don't use them often enough and they quickly turn rancid. I compensate by adding actual chopped nuts—walnuts, hazelnuts or pecans—directly to the salad, imparting the "nutty" flavor I want to achieve. If you do purchase a nut oil, store it in the refrigerator for a longer life.

FLAVOR ENHANCERS

These ingredients can help balance or deepen the flavor of dressings.

Shallots

Finely minced shallots can almost always be added to your dressing, and they lend an aromatic depth that's a little more subtle than that of garlic or onions. Their mild flavor permeates the vinaigrette, and they're ideal to use when the taste of garlic would be overpowering. One teaspoon to 1 tablespoon of finely minced shallot is usually enough. Chop—or even grate—the shallot as finely as possible. You can use a Microplane grater.

Garlic

A clove of minced raw or roasted garlic also adds plenty of flavor, especially to Italian, Caesar, Greek or herb vinaigrettes. Try combining shallots and garlic for a more robust flavor.

Mustard

A creamy mustard such as Dijon adds a sharp flavor that's not unlike that of vinegar. It also acts as a binder that helps emulsify a vinaigrette. Add 1 teaspoon to 1 tablespoon of mustard, tasting as you go.

Fresh and Dried Herbs and Spices

Salad-friendly fresh herbs like basil, parsley, oregano, cilantro, dill, chives, chervil and mint add freshness and extra flavor, either in the dressing or directly on top of the salad. Adding 1 tablespoon of a fresh herb is a good starting point; you can always add more to taste. Dried herbs and spices that are salad-friendly include oregano, cumin, coriander, curry powder, paprika or cayenne for a little heat. In this case, 1/2 to 1 teaspoon is usually enough for flavor, with the exception of cayenne, a pinch to 1/4 teaspoon of which will suffice.

Sugar, Honey, Brown Sugar and Maple Syrup

A touch of sweetness is another way to round out a vinaigrette, usually mellowing the tang of the vinegar to some degree. A teaspoon or two of maple syrup or honey, or a pinch of sugar can all do the trick. I do this often, rather than add more oil to balance a dressing. I've also found that adding crumbled blue cheese or feta cheese to a salad can mellow a too-sharp vinaigrette.

Citrus or fruit juice can be mixed in to help cut back on olive oil. Adding 1 to 4 tablespoons of freshly squeezed orange juice or red grapefruit juice adds a delicious flavor to vinaigrettes.

Because the citrus juices are water-based, these dressings can wilt a salad more quickly than regular vinaigrettes and are best added just before serving.

Kosher Salt

Of the three basic salts (table, sea and kosher), kosher salt yields the best results in salads. Most vinaigrette recipes suggest adding salt and pepper "to taste." A dressing for 4 servings of salad made with 2 tablespoons of vinegar and 5 of olive oil gets 2 to 3 pinches of kosher salt (about 1/4 to 1/2 teaspoon). If a vinaigrette tastes bland, adding more salt can usually help. Most vinaigrettes also benefit from pepper, freshly ground right into the mix.

Other

Try these interesting new twists:

- **Anchovies**
- **Horseradish**
- **Olives**
- **Jalapeño peppers**
- **Lemongrass**
- **Sun-dried tomatoes**
- **Grated citrus zests**

These additions go directly into the oil-vinegar mix; the more they are finely minced—almost to a paste—the more the flavor will be evenly distributed throughout.

BASIC RED WINE VINAIGRETTE

Using a basic formula of 1 tablespoon of vinegar to 3 tablespoons olive oil, you can vary vinegars—apple cider, white vinegar, Champagne vinegars—depending on the dressing that will best complement your salad. You may need more or less olive oil to counterbalance the strength of each type of vinegar. For basic variations or additions such as shallots, garlic and herbs, see page 243.

2 tablespoons red wine vinegar
1/2 teaspoon Dijon mustard
6 to 7 tablespoons olive oil
2 good pinches or about 1/4 teaspoon
  kosher salt
Pepper

1 In a small bowl, whisk together the red wine vinegar and mustard. Add the oil in a slow, steady stream, whisking constantly. Season with salt and pepper.

BASIL-BALSAMIC VINAIGRETTE

Because this dressing is so tasty and fresh basil is available all year long, I don't wait until summer anymore to make it. It's especially delicious on green salads with tomatoes and other garden-fresh additions.

3 tablespoons balsamic vinegar
1/4 teaspoon finely minced garlic
1/3 cup lightly packed fresh basil leaves
1/2 cup olive oil
2 generous pinches of salt
Pepper

1 Place the vinegar, garlic, basil, half of the oil, 2 pinches of salt and pepper in a blender. Blend until basil is incorporated. Add the remaining oil and pulse once or twice to emulsify.

VARIATION To make a lemon-basil vinaigrette, substitute 3 tablespoons of fresh lemon juice for the balsamic vinegar.

MAPLE-BALSAMIC VINAIGRETTE

This is my "go-to" balsamic dressing. My trick to making it special is adding a touch of real maple syrup. It thickens and balances the vinegar so that it tastes like its long-aged, expensive cousins.

3 tablespoons balsamic vinegar
2 teaspoons maple syrup
2 teaspoons minced shallot
1 teaspoon Dijon mustard
1/2 cup olive oil
Salt and pepper

1 In a small bowl, whisk together the vinegar, maple syrup, shallot and mustard. Add the oil, whisking constantly. Season with salt and pepper.

VARIATIONS This dressing is wonderful with the addition of 10 to 12 fresh basil leaves as well as a few pitted black olives, either solo or in combination with the basil. I suggest making both of these variations in a blender to thoroughly incorporate the basil and olives. If you do, add the oil at the very end and briefly pulse to combine.

GREEN GODDESS DRESSING

Try this beautiful green dressing over almost any greens, on tomatoes, as a sauce over fish or chicken, or as a dip for vegetables. This is a good dressing to experiment with, and try all kinds of variations with: other fresh herbs, including tarragon and chives; adding minced anchovies or garlic, or even lime juice and cilantro for a slightly Southwestern flavor.

1/4 cup plain yogurt (preferably whole milk)
1/3 cup mayonnaise
1 tablespoon minced shallot
1 tablespoon fresh lemon juice
1/4 cup chopped fresh herbs such as a
  basil, dill and/or parsley
Salt and pepper

1 Place all of the dressing ingredients in a food processor or blender and process until the dressing is creamy and herbs are incorporated.

MAKES ABOUT 3/4 CUP

ITALIAN HERB VINAIGRETTE

Here is a great multi-purpose salad dressing for the times you want to toss up a salad with many different ingredients, including leafy greens, grains and vegetables. It goes well with everything.

2 tablespoons red wine vinegar or apple cider vinegar

2 teaspoons fresh lemon juice

1 teaspoon Dijon mustard

1/2 teaspoon each dried oregano, basil and thyme

1 medium clove garlic, finely minced

1/2 cup olive oil

Salt and pepper

1 In a small bowl, whisk together the vinegar, lemon juice, mustard, herbs and garlic. Add the oil in a thin, steady stream, whisking constantly. Season with salt and pepper.

MAKES ABOUT 3/4 CUP

REDUCED ORANGE VINAIGRETTE

Use flavorful oranges such as tangerines or blood oranges for this dressing; the juice is reduced, yielding a wonderful, concentrated taste. Try it on bitter or spicy greens like arugula, radicchio or watercress, and salads with beets, avocado, citrus or fruit. You can lighten it up by substituting Champagne or Moscatel vinegar for the balsamic or red wine vinegar. If you don't have time to reduce the orange juice, just decrease the amount to 3 or 4 tablespoons.

1 cup fresh orange juice

1 teaspoon grated orange zest

2 tablespoons balsamic vinegar or red wine vinegar

2 teaspoons finely minced shallot or red onion

6 tablespoons olive oil

2 pinches of salt

1 Place orange juice in a small saucepan and bring to a boil. Lower the heat and simmer, uncovered, until juice is reduced to 1/4 cup. Remove from heat and let cool slightly.

2 In a small bowl, combine the orange zest, balsamic or red wine vinegar and shallot. Slowly add the oil, whisking constantly. Add reduced juice and salt to taste; whisk again.

MAKES ABOUT 3/4 CUP

GREEK HERB VINAIGRETTE

Among my favorite versatile dressings is this quick and easy-to-make Greek vinaigrette. Adding a touch of citrus to a vinegar-based dressing gives it a bright taste. Try tossing this with romaine salads, Greek salads, or on any mesclun salad mixes, as well as with pasta or vegetable salads.

2 tablespoons red wine vinegar

2 teaspoons fresh lemon juice

1 teaspoon dried oregano or 2 teaspoons fresh oregano

1/2 teaspoon minced garlic

1/2 cup olive oil

Salt and pepper

1 In a small bowl, whisk together the vinegar, lemon juice, oregano and garlic. Whisk in the oil, whisking constantly. Season with salt and pepper.

MAKES ABOUT 1/2 CUP

249
·
RAISING
THE
SALAD
BAR
·

APPLE CIDER-HONEY VINAIGRETTE

Try this dressing on leafy green salads that include fruit and/or cheese.

2 tablespoons apple cider vinegar
1 teaspoon finely minced shallot
1 to 1 & 1/2 teaspoons honey
6 tablespoons olive oil
Salt and pepper

1 In a small bowl, whisk together the vinegar, shallot and honey. Add the oil in a slow, steady stream, whisking constantly. Season with salt and pepper.

APPLE CIDER VINEGAR AND HEALTH My mother often talked about the health benefits of sipping a little apple cider vinegar with water each day, and my friend Sarah Vail swears it wards off sickness. While putting this book together, Sarah and I learned that the oldest woman in the U.S. credits using apple cider vinegar in everything she makes for her longevity.

MAKES ABOUT 1/2 CUP

LEMON-LIME CITRUS DRESSING

Serve this dressing with broiled or grilled fish, or with vegetable salads such as asparagus, broccoli or cauliflower.

6 tablespoons olive oil
1 tablespoon capers, rinsed
1 tablespoon fresh lemon juice
1 tablespoon fresh lime juice
1/2 teaspoon minced garlic
1 tablespoon minced fresh parsley
Salt and pepper

1 In a small saucepan, heat 1 tablespoon of the oil over medium heat. Add the capers and let them sizzle for 2 or 3 minutes. Remove pan from heat and let cool. In a small bowl, whisk together the lemon and lime juices, garlic, parsley and remaining 5 tablespoons oil. Season with salt and pepper, then add the capers, including the oil they cooked in. Adjust the seasonings and add additional citrus if needed.

MAKES ABOUT 1 CUP

FRESH HERB VINAIGRETTE

This is a good multi-purpose vinaigrette to have on hand. You can vary the flavor by adding your choice of fresh herbs. I usually mix two or three herbs, if I have them, but you can also use lots of just dill for a potato and green bean salad; basil and parsley for a tomato or bean salad, and so on. After the first day, green herbs lose their color, but their good taste remains.

1/4 cup red wine or white wine vinegar
1 tablespoon finely minced shallot
1 clove garlic, finely minced
3/4 cup olive oil
1/2 teaspoon kosher salt
Pepper
1/3 cup minced fresh parsley, dill, basil, oregano, chives or cilantro

1 In a small bowl, whisk together the vinegar, shallot and garlic. Whisk in the oil until dressing is smooth and creamy. Season with salt and pepper and add the fresh herbs. Taste and adjust seasonings if necessary.

MAKES 1/2 CUP

LEMON-SESAME DRESSING

In the mood for something different? Try this—it's good with any kind of lettuce, or with green salads that include vegetables such as cucumbers, tomatoes, avocados and red onions. Sprinkle toasted sesame seeds on top of the salad for additional flavor. Drawn from the classic Middle Eastern tahini dressing, this version can be served with falafel, kababs and pita-stuffed sandwiches, too.

2 tablespoons fresh lemon juice
1 tablespoon tahini
2 teaspoons soy sauce
1/2 teaspoon minced garlic
1/4 cup olive oil
1 tablespoon minced parsley
Salt and pepper, to taste

1 In a small bowl, whisk together all of the dressing ingredients, mixing well to combine.

VARIATION Add 1 teaspoon ground cumin and/or 1/4 teaspoon cayenne

MAKES ABOUT 1 CUP

251
·
RAISING
THE
SALAD
BAR
·

VIETNAMESE LIME-CHILE DRESSING

When I think about the chefs and friends I've known who make outstanding salads and slaws, at the top of the list is Boston chef Didi Emmons, author of the best-selling books *Vegetarian Planet* and *Entertaining for a Veggie Planet*. With this vibrant, spicy dressing, she never disappoints. She suggests playing with salad combinations such as sliced red cabbage, blanched green beans, unsweetened coconut, sprouts and chopped roasted peanuts; or black quinoa, mizuna or mesclun greens, diced tart apple and roasted peanuts. Grated carrot and thinly sliced red onion would be good additions, too.

1 tablespoon brown sugar
1 clove garlic, minced
1 teaspoon chile sauce, or more to taste
1/2 cup fresh mint leaves
1/4 cup fresh lime juice
2/3 cup canola oil
Salt or Asian fish sauce

1 In a blender, combine the brown sugar, garlic, chile sauce, mint leaves and lime juice until the mint is finely chopped. Add the oil slowly from the top of the blender while it's still running; add a large pinch of salt or a dash of fish sauce, to taste. Blend until the dressing is creamy.

CHILE SAUCE Didi suggests the sambal oelek chile paste made by Huy Fong Foods (with a rooster on the label). You can also use sriracha chili sauce, made by the same company, which is a spicy, thick Asian hot sauce made from red chiles and vinegar.

MAKES ABOUT 3/4 CUP

CILANTRO-LIME VINAIGRETTE

The combination of lime juice and cilantro makes a good dressing. You can toss the jalapeño pepper and garlic clove into the blender, which does all the work in this recipe. Enjoy this on green salads with chicken, as a sauce for fish, or to dress up a rice or bean salad.

4 tablespoons fresh lime juice
1 jalapeño pepper, cored and seeded
1 clove garlic
1/4 cup lightly packed cilantro
1/2 cup olive oil
Salt and pepper

1 In a blender, combine the lime juice, jalapeño pepper, garlic, cilantro and oil. Blend until dressing is creamy. Add salt and pepper to taste.

VARIATION You can easily turn this dressing into a spicy Cumin-Lime Vinaigrette. Reduce the amount of cilantro to 1 or 2 tablespoons and add 1 teaspoon ground cumin. Whisk the dressing, rather than blend it. Try it on leafy green salads or salads with avocado, corn, fennel, orange and fruit. For an extra-spicy version, I add 1 chipotle pepper from a can of chipotle peppers in adobo sauce and blend well.

MAKES ABOUT 1/2 CUP

CREAMY LEMON-WALNUT DRESSING

The smooth sweetness of this walnut dressing is perfect with baby greens or slightly bitter lettuces like watercress, arugula, dandelion, endive or radicchio. It's also nice with salads that are garnished with fruit. You can decrease the olive oil by 1 or 2 tablespoons and add the same amount of walnut oil for added nut flavor, if desired.

1/3 cup walnuts
3 tablespoons fresh lemon juice
1/2 teaspoon dry mustard
1 teaspoon maple syrup or honey
3 tablespoons olive oil
Salt and pepper

1 To toast the walnuts, preheat the oven to 350°. Place nuts on a baking sheet and roast for 7 to 9 minutes. Remove from oven and let cool. Rub the cooled nuts with your hands or place in a cotton towel to remove as much brown skin as possible.

2 Place the toasted walnuts in a blender and process until they're finely chopped. Add 2 tablespoons water, the lemon juice, dry mustard, maple syrup, oil, and salt and pepper; blend until dressing is creamy. If it's too thick, add more water, 1 teaspoon at a time.

MAKES ABOUT 2/3 CUP

BLUE CHEESE DRESSING

Try this dressing over any of the heartier greens, or with grilled beef salads. It's also delicious over potato salad.

1/4 cup blue cheese
2 tablespoons crème fraîche, heavy cream or milk
2 tablespoons fresh lemon juice
5 tablespoons olive oil
1/4 teaspoon kosher salt
Pepper

1 Place the blue cheese, cream or milk, lemon juice and oil in a food processor. Process until dressing is creamy; season with salt and pepper. If you don't own a food processor, in a small bowl, mash together the blue cheese, cream and lemon juice. Whisk in the oil until dressing is creamy. Season with salt and pepper.

GREMOLATA VINAIGRETTE

Gremolata is a robust combination of lemon zest, parsley and garlic that is usually served with meat or fish dishes. Here it's made into a vinaigrette that makes a delicious dressing for salads with grains or beans, and vegetables and greens such as watercress or mizuna. It also pairs well with cooked vegetables.

1 teaspoon grated lemon zest
1 clove garlic, finely minced
1 teaspoon Dijon mustard
1/2 teaspoon honey
2 tablespoons fresh lemon juice
5 tablespoons olive oil
1 tablespoon minced fresh parsley
Salt and pepper

1 In a small bowl, whisk together the lemon zest, garlic, mustard, honey and lemon juice. Whisk in the oil until dressing is thick and creamy. Add the parsley, salt and pepper; whisk again.

CREAMY ITALIAN DRESSING

This tangy, smooth dressing can adorn any kind of leafy green mix. It goes especially well with romaine or arugula, or Cobb salad with chicken. You can choose to leave out the cheese. In that case, add another tablespoon of yogurt or cream. This dressing likes lots of freshly ground pepper.

3 tablespoons fresh lemon juice
1/2 teaspoon minced garlic
2 tablespoons heavy cream, sour cream,
  crème fraîche or plain yogurt
6 tablespoons olive oil
2 tablespoons grated Parmigiano Reggiano
Salt and pepper

1 In a small bowl, whisk together the lemon juice, garlic, and cream or yogurt. In a thin, steady stream, whisk in the olive oil until dressing is creamy. Add the Parmesan cheese, salt and lots of pepper. You can also prepare this dressing in a food processor or blender, adding the oil last and pulsing a few times to thoroughly incorporate it.

MAKES 3/4 CUP

CLASSIC CAESAR SALAD DRESSING

Creamy, lemony and delicious, this classic dressing can take on almost any type of salad. If using a raw egg bothers you, try the very similar Lemon-Anchovy dressing, Creamy Italian dressing, or read the note below. If you choose to use eggs, add 1 or 2 egg yolks, depending on how thick you like your dressing.

1 or 2 egg yolks
3 anchovy fillets
1/2 teaspoon minced garlic
1 teaspoon Dijon mustard
3 tablespoons fresh lemon juice
1/2 cup olive oil
Salt and pepper

1 Place the egg yolks, anchovies, garlic, mustard and lemon juice in a food processor and process thoroughly. With the food processor still running, add the oil. Season the dressing with salt and pepper, then pulse to combine the ingredients.

2 If you don't own a food processor, mince the anchovy fillets and place in a small bowl. Whisk in the egg yolk, garlic, mustard and lemon juice. Whisk in the oil in a thin, steady stream. Season with salt and pepper.

COOKING EGGS FOR CAESAR SALAD If you're concerned about raw eggs as a food safety issue, there is a way to slightly cook the egg yolks before using them for a Caesar salad: Bring a small saucepan of water to a simmer. Carefully add the whole egg in its shell and cook for 2 minutes. Remove with a slotted spoon and crack the yolk into a small bowl. Discard the egg white.

SERVES 4

LEMON-ANCHOVY DRESSING
(EGG-FREE CAESAR SALAD DRESSING)

This is a wonderful, simple, lemony dressing that gets its depth of flavor from anchovies. Don't be afraid to try them—you will be surprised. Once blended into the mixture, there is no discernible anchovy or "fishy" taste at all. The trinity of anchovy, lemon and garlic forms the basis of a Caesar salad dressing, so I consider this akin to an egg-less version. Use it with greens, vegetables or potatoes, too. I usually use this dressing on the day I make it.

3 anchovy fillets
1/2 teaspoon minced garlic
1 teaspoon Dijon mustard
3 tablespoons fresh lemon juice
1/2 cup olive oil
Salt and pepper

1 Place the anchovies, garlic, mustard and lemon juice in a food processor and process thoroughly. Stop the processor, add the olive oil, salt and pepper, and pulse to combine. If you don't own a food processor, mince the anchovy fillets and place in a bowl; whisk in the garlic, mustard, lemon juice and oil. Season with salt and pepper.

MAKES ABOUT 1 CUP

SUNFLOWER SEED-FLAX DRESSING

Full of good flavor and nutrition, this versatile blender-made dressing comes from natural-foods cooking coach Chris Brown of Warren, Rhode Island. Our paths usually cross at the inspirational Crystal Spring Center for Earth Literacy in Plainville, Massachusetts where we both teach cooking classes.

1/2 cup raw hulled sunflower seeds
1/2 cup water
3 tablespoons fresh lemon juice
2 tablespoons olive oil
2 tablespoons flaxseed oil
1 tablespoon soy sauce
1 teaspoon dried tarragon
1 teaspoon dried dill
1 or 2 minced cloves garlic

1 Grind the sunflower seeds in a blender until they are powdered. Add the remaining ingredients and continue to blend until dressing is smooth.

 FLAX SEED OIL Flax seed oil contains the highly recommended omega 6 oils, also found in certain fish like salmon. Flaxseed oil can be found in natural foods markets. It should be stored in the refrigerator and used mostly in salads, as heating it destroys some of its nutritional qualities.

MAKES ABOUT 1 CUP

TOMATO-OLIVE VINAIGRETTE

Luscious olives, sweet tomatoes and fresh lemon juice make a sumptuous dressing that can be spooned over fish on a bed of greens. It also works beautifully on green salads, pasta salads, and grain or bean salads. Vary the flavor by substituting fresh dill, tarragon or basil for the parsley.

2 tablespoons red wine vinegar

2 tablespoons fresh lemon juice

1/4 teaspoon minced garlic

2/3 cup olive oil

1/2 cup seeded tomatoes, cut into 1/4-inch dice

3 tablespoons chopped, pitted kalamata olives

1 tablespoon minced fresh parsley

Salt and pepper

1 In a medium bowl, whisk the vinegar, lemon juice and garlic. Slowly whisk in the oil. Add chopped tomatoes, olives, parsley, and salt and pepper; mix well. Leftover dressing can be refrigerated for up to 3 days.

VARIATION To make an all-tomato vinaigrette, simply omit the olives and add more fresh herbs, especially fresh basil and parsley.

MAKES ABOUT 2/3 CUP

HONEY-MUSTARD VINAIGRETTE

This is a nicely balanced dressing for chicken, greens, potatoes or fish.

2 tablespoons apple cider vinegar

1 tablespoon Dijon mustard

2 to 3 teaspoons honey

1 clove garlic, minced

1/2 cup olive oil

1/2 teaspoon kosher salt

Pepper

1 In a small bowl, whisk together the vinegar, mustard, honey and garlic, then whisk in the oil. Season with salt and pepper.

MAKES ABOUT 1/2 CUP

259
·
RAISING
THE
SALAD
BAR
·

GRAPEFRUIT VINAIGRETTE

This is a light and fruity vinaigrette that gets its fresh flavor from grapefruit juice. When you use citrus, you can usually cut back on oil. Try this dressing with mixed leafy greens. It goes especially well with peppery arugula and watercress, and green salads topped with citrus sections and avocado slices.

1/4 cup fresh pink grapefruit juice
1 tablespoon Champagne vinegar, or other light vinegar such as rice vinegar, Moscatel or raspberry
1 teaspoon minced shallot
2 tablespoons olive oil
2 pinches salt

1 In a small bowl, whisk the grapefruit juice, vinegar and shallot. Whisk in the oil and 2 pinches of salt. Because citrus dressings don't really emulsify, whisk the mixture again just before dressing the salad.

ASIAN VINAIGRETTE

Use this versatile, Asian-flavored dressing for leafy green salads, Asian greens, or slaws, pasta salads and vegetables. When purchasing rice vinegar, pick an unseasoned one, that is, without sugar or salt.

1 tablespoon rice vinegar
2 tablespoons fresh lime or lemon juice
1 tablespoon maple syrup or honey
1 teaspoon finely-minced fresh ginger
1 tablespoon soy sauce
3 tablespoons canola or grapeseed oil
1 tablespoon toasted sesame oil

1 In a small bowl, whisk together the rice vinegar, citrus juice, maple syrup or honey, ginger, soy sauce, canola oil and sesame oil. Just before dressing the salad, whisk the mixture again to emulsify the ingredients.

MAKES ABOUT 3/4 CUP

RASPBERRY VINAIGRETTE

This is a light, fresh-tasting vinaigrette with a pretty pink hue. Use raspberry vinegar if you have it. Because of the fresh raspberries in this dressing, other vinegars like apple cider, rice wine vinegar or Champagne vinegar would also be fine. Try this with a light coleslaw, as well as salads with spicy greens. It's also delicious with salads that include fruits and berries, such as raspberries, blackberries, melons or orange sections.

2 tablespoons raspberry or other light vinegar
1/4 cup fresh or frozen raspberries
2 tablespoons fresh orange juice
2 teaspoons honey
6 tablespoons olive oil
Salt

1 Place the raspberry vinegar, raspberries, orange juice and honey in a blender; blend to combine. Add the oil and pulse to incorporate it. Add salt to taste.

MAKES ABOUT 1 CUP

RASPBERRY-ORANGE VINAIGRETTE

This is a light, fruity vinaigrette that cuts back on olive oil by using freshly squeezed orange juice.

3 tablespoons raspberry or Moscatel vinegar
1/3 cup fresh orange juice
1 teaspoon maple syrup, honey or other sweetener
1 teaspoon Dijon mustard
1 tablespoon minced shallot or red onion
6 tablespoons olive oil
1/4 teaspoon kosher salt

1 Combine the raspberry vinegar, orange juice, maple syrup or honey, mustard, shallots, oil and salt in a blender. Blend until shallots or onion are pureed.

MANGO SALSA VINAIGRETTE

A cross between a salsa and a vinaigrette, this mango dressing is wonderful spooned over fish or chicken nestled in salad greens. Don't pass it by without trying it!

1 ripe mango
2 tablespoons red wine vinegar
2 tablespoons fresh lime juice
1 & 1/2 teaspoons honey
6 tablespoons olive oil
2 tablespoons minced red onion
1/2 teaspoon minced garlic
1/2 teaspoon ground cumin
1/2 cup seeded and finely diced tomato
1/4 teaspoon kosher salt
2 to 3 tablespoons chopped cilantro leaves

1 To prepare the mango, peel off the skin with a vegetable peeler or paring knife. Slice off a little of the bottom so that you can easily hold the mango upright. Make three or four 1/4-inch thick slices down either side of the pit. Cut each slice into 1/4-inch strips, and each strip into 1/4-inch dice. Set aside 1 cup of diced mango, save the rest for another use.

2 In a medium bowl, combine the vinegar, lime juice and honey. Add the oil in a thin stream, whisking constantly to emulsify. Add the red onion, garlic, cumin, mango, tomato and salt; combine well. Stir in the cilantro leaves. If you're not serving the salad immediately, store this dressing in the refrigerator, but bring it to room temperature before using.

SOURCES

262
·
RAISING
THE
SALAD
BAR
·

These are some of my favorite sources for vinegar, spices and other specialty food items.

HERBS

Penzeys Spices
Brookfield, Wisconsin
www.penzeys.com
(800) 741-7787
• Full line of regular and hard-to-find herbs and spices.

VINEGARS

Cheshire Garden
Winchester, New Hampshire
www.cheshiregarden.com
(800) 597-7822
• Herbal and fruit vinegars; farmhouse mustards.

O Olive Oil Company
San Rafael, California
www.ooliveoil.com
(888) 827-7148
• O Brand Vinegars including Cabernet, Zinfandel, Sherry, Champagne, PortO etc.

The Shelburne Apple Co.
Shelburne, Massachusetts
(413) 625-2744
• Apple Cider Vinegar from 100 percent farm-fresh cider.

Sparrow Lane Vineyards
Angwin, California
www.sparrowlane.com
(707) 815-1813
• Varietal Napa Valley aged vinegars, white balsamic and fruit vinegars.

St. Helena Olive Oil Company
Rutherford, California
www.sholiveoil.com
(800) 939-9880
• Varietal wine vinegars, including Champagne and Cabernet Sauvignon vinegar.

Whole Foods Markets
To find the Whole Foods Market nearest you, visit www.wholefoods.com
• Specialty vinegars (Unio Moscatel Vinegar, Villa Manodori Aceto Balsamico di Modena), including their own balsamic brand, Whole Foods 365 Balsamic.

INDEX

INDEX

264
·
RAISING
THE
SALAD
BAR
·

INDEX

266

·

RAISING
THE
SALAD
BAR

·

INDEX

270
•
RAISING
THE
SALAD
BAR
•

INDEX

272
·
RAISING
THE
SALAD
BAR
·